THE POET'S
QUEST
FOR GOD

EYEWEAR PUBLISHING

Edited by
FR. OLIVER BRENNAN
& TODD SWIFT
with KELLY DAVIO
& CATE MYDDLETON-EVANS
Introduction by EWAN FERNIE

THE POET'S QUEST FOR GOD

21ST CENTURY POEMS OF FAITH, DOUBT AND WONDER

First published in 2016
by Eyewear Publishing Ltd
Suite 333, 19-21 Crawford Street
Marylebone, London W1H 1PJ
United Kingdom

Typeset with graphic design by Edwin Smet
Printed in England by TJ International Ltd, Padstow, Cornwall

ISBN 978-1-908998-25-5

*Eyewear wishes to thank Jonathan Wonham for his generous patronage
of our press.*

*As this anthology represents many international uses of 'English', we have
chosen not to impose one standard; therefore, spelling may vary accordingly.*

*Every attempt has been made to avoid any errors in these texts, and any that
have cropped in are the sole responsibility of the editors; in some instances,
variations of typography or sense which might seem eccentric are intended
poetic choices.*

*The poets appear in a chiefly alphabetic order, starting, nicely, with Abell
and ending with Zieroth.*

WWW.EYEWEARPUBLISHING.COM

DEDICATED TO

Sebastian Barker (1945-2014)

TABLE OF CONTENTS

EDITORIAL PREFACE

This book arose out of a series of conversations between the editors, Todd Swift and Fr. Oliver Brennan, that began in the late 1990s. Fr. Brennan, educated at Fordham University in America as a scholar of the dynamics of Religious Faith and Culture, but also by then a Parish Priest in the Archdiocese of Armagh, was interested in weaving in poems into his homilies during Mass – often quoting post-modern poets, many of whom were far from being apologists for Christianity.

As Fr. Brennan once wrote: 'one of the characteristics of contemporary culture, generally described as post-modern, is the human search for the spiritual. Many spiritual writers say that desire is our fundamental dis-ease and is always stronger than satisfaction. This desire lies at the centre of our lives, deep in the recesses of the soul. The unquenchable fire residing in all of us manifests itself at key points in the human life-cycle. Spirituality is ultimately what we do about this desire'.

Swift, a poet, became intrigued by this idea of desire and how poems far exceeded their own places and times and felt useful, inspiring and valuable to persons wishing to be comforted or supported in their spiritual questing. So the initial aim was to establish an anthology of contemporary poems that a Christian reader would learn from and enjoy. This became too limiting a frame. The editors found many poets and poems of the Jewish, Muslim, Buddhist or Hindu traditions that they also wanted to include. Soon they recognised that poems about God, the possibility of God, or the absence of God, far from being rare, were everywhere – a rich orchard waiting to be picked.

Brennan and Swift began to meet regularly in Co. Louth, Ireland and London, England, in hotels by roaring fires and in homes at kitchen tables, reading vast numbers of poems over sandwiches and tea. Great discussions and debates ensued, but also much enjoyment. The editors felt fortunate to have this project and this time of friendship and calm to pursue it. They began to conceive of a diverse and multifaceted house, where belief, interpretation, seeking, questioning and objection were welcome. And so they put out a call for poems by people of all faiths, or none.

★

The anthology, as it developed, opened up a dialogue with all those searching for a deeper spiritual awareness, a search that for some may lead to explicit belief in God. We live in a violent, visual world, where what is most valued is that which we can see, measure, physically touch, scientifically prove and logically explain. We cannot prove that God exists in a scientific, logical sense but few things that really matter can be proven that way. You cannot prove that somebody loves you using science. But you can know in your heart and mind that love exists and is real. *The invisible can be just as real as the visible* – a shared core belief of most religions and much poetry.

Human beings not only act violently towards each other but also towards the fragile planet which is their only place of habitation (except in the case of a few astronauts) during their earthly journey. Good poetry and authentic religion might be stays against this violence, more often than instigators (though for some critics of either or both, this is not the case). Poetry and religion can be natural friends, if only because poetry is, or leads to, inner thought, imaginative reaching, mindfulness, reflection, meditation, prayer and at times a more harmonious way of living with the environment and other humans.

Poetry, of course, is not always 'good' or healthy (one thinks of Baudelaire, Dylan Thomas and Plath as beacons of the shadow side of poetic power) but then the forces unleashed by religions are also complex, ambiguous and creatively fraught, in history and human time, as measured against the transcendent. We hope to emphasise here poetry in balance with life, love and nature as much as it may have been born in chaos, but do not seek to limit the power and vitality of either poem or religious thought, allowing what some may consider the negative or the darkness to meet the light.

Respecting that the values shared by the major world religions are greater than the ways in which they may differ, the editors of this anthology began to recognise enough of substance, continuity and community to see the book's threads intertwine firmly, a tapestry formed of darkness and light, hope and doubt, awe and humility, anger and gratitude.

To raise a fist at the sky and demand God appear and solve problems of sorrow, horror and loss, from Job to yesterday in any one of the world's shattering war zones, is not childish or less valid than to praise God for the shape of good things discernible against a visibly dark backdrop. To deny is sometimes even to ask for, or bring to the horizon of the possible. The impossible is handmaiden to the discovered. We began to see a poetic quest as a dance along a very varied and fertile spectrum.

We hope that by opening up the book to poems that are by craft or by purpose abstract and direct, brutal and sensually subtle, overtly for and overtly against the notion of faith, belief or God, the anthology provides a relatively broad representation of such a response. As editors, we have not only been blessed by the variety of poetics, but also by the weight and quality of submissions. Since the window was opened in early 2012 to when it was finally, reluctantly, clapped shut in early 2016, Eyewear Publishing has received over two thousand poems.

What was incredible to see was the way in which, like trees passing the first breeze of spring between their leaves, the word of the anthology spread. We would often receive e-mails from poet friends of other poets, of associates of other poets, of mild acquaintances of those poets who had first received the call. And while the vast majority of the poets included here are previously published, even well-known, what the length and openness of the window has enabled us to do is to extract gems (sometimes by emerging poets) that otherwise would not have been found.

Along the way, this book became massive, with many moving parts, and it became necessary to ask for assistance from junior editors who gladly joined the project and then in turn moved on. They are therefore to be thanked here: Dominic Bury, Cate Myddleton-Evans and Kelly Davio all helped to make this book possible (as did hundreds of people who pre-ordered the book to allow us to keep going when it seemed, for a time, that funding for the project might run out). Few anthologies of modern times have been so anticipated, supported, or delayed – but here it is and not a moment too soon.

In February 2016, viewers of the new version of *The X-Files* – whose themes of belief and doubt are infamous – would have seen a conversation between the characters Mulder and Scully, debating the possibility of the existence of God in a world apparently riven by love and hate, war and peace. If anything, the rise of new terror cells and new demagogues (in America and beyond) has led to more editorials, articles, books, tweets and posts about religion and its implications than ever before.

It is for this world that this book was prepared. There is perhaps no other book quite like it (yet) but hopefully there will be more. Here are great poems jostling together to reinvent and shape the way we think about, read, imagine and consider both poetry, and the search for spiritual truths beyond (or almost beyond) mortal ken, human desire.

THE EDITORS
6 June, 2016
Maida Vale, London

NOTE: For a variety of reasons, it was decided to leave out biographical notes at the end of the anthology. These include wanting to leave more room for poems (even brief bios took up 25 pages at one stage); an interest in emphasing poem over information easily accessed now by the Internet; and the difficulty of revising so many biographies that were constantly in flux. Suffice it to say, all the poets were living at the time of inclusion, though sadly, a few have died since the book began.

INTRODUCTION BY EWAN FERNIE

I'm an academic in English studies and I recall, some years ago
now, being at the big American conference in my discipline
(this will become pertinent, I promise...). It's one of the best
conferences. Everyone who's anyone goes, it's held in a big
attractive city, there's a sense of expectancy about what'll happen,
what the new thing will prove to be, who you might meet or
dine with, etc. And of course you're getting away from your
more mundane duties back home. No doubt that year was just as
good as always. But, sitting in another miscellaneous ballroom,
under what suddenly felt like a pompous chandelier, I was bored
and alienated. A failure of attention and, indeed, charity in me
– I doubt I would've felt the same had I been the one speaking.
Still, I couldn't shake it: a feeling that the conference wasn't
doing what the best literature does, that it wasn't communicating
with what my friend Jonathan Dollimore calls 'the Big Stuff'
– life, meaning, value. I suppose that these things were being
indirectly invoked all the time, but literature makes you *feel* them.
One way or another, it makes you more alive. At the same time
as I was struggling on my comfy seat with these (admittedly, not
very original) reflections, it struck me that we were supposedly
in the middle of one of the world's great religious festivals,
that tomorrow was Easter Sunday. By the time I'd got out of
the ballroom I was determined not to spend another evening
networking and talking shop. Instead I went, on my own, to hear
the Brahms *Requiem*. I was quickly swept up into its scriptural
but strictly this-worldly struggle with life and death. It seemed
so luxurious, and not only because it was so full and sensuous an
experience after so much criticism. It also somehow restored me
to a deep source of peace and energy in myself. Yes, peace as well
as energy, in spite or perhaps actually because of all the *Requiem*'s
honest turbulence.... The next morning I went to the Cathedral
to experience the thing Brahms so pointedly refused to write: the
Catholic Mass. I'm not a Catholic, but it still seemed the most

natural thing to do, before, during and after. Returning to the conference hotel to pack up and check out, I met a friendly colleague in the lobby. She asked where I'd been that morning and the night before and I told her, and she asked if I was having a mid-life crisis.

That anecdote might help suggest why I think *The Poet's Quest For God* represents a brave and necessary intervention in our culture. This book reconnects two things through which men and women have often sought life, meaning and value, and it reconnects them to the potential betterment and strengthening of both. It does so in the context of a literate culture that hasn't really 'got' religion for some time. But religion hasn't gone away. Most would have said till recently that we were living in religion's last days, but it now sometimes seems as though we might be on the cusp of its new dawn. In avant-garde contemporary theory, for instance, all the big guns, from Jacques Derrida to Slavoj Žižek, have been busily exhuming the God many of them gleefully brought down. A comparable surprise is that the most intellectually energetic form of contemporary Christian theology is the so-called Radical Orthodoxy movement. Or maybe this isn't surprising: orthodoxy may have become freshly thinkable as a system precisely because it has been culturally denaturalised. Still, at a more popular level, our times have equally seen the unpredictable rise of evangelical fundamentalism. At the same time, a major outbreak of unchurched 'spirituality' is forking in the other direction: a phenomenon which, according to many commentators, is too privatised, self-serving and inchoate to be taken seriously, particularly in the context of the intense, sometimes murderous politicisation of religion in global politics, at home and abroad. But even if they're right, contemporary spirituality at least testifies to a widespread hunger for something more than ordinary life offers.

In such a complex situation, it's difficult to get your bearings. And that old chestnut that we should really just avoid the topic at all costs starts to look like real wisdom again. But if politeness circumvents embarrassment and argument in the short term, it leaves some serious issues begging. How should we relate to our religious inheritance? What to do about latent or insurgent religiosity in and beyond our societies? And if we're to do away with religion, won't we create a need for something else? After all, even a concept so culturally remote as salvation actually does a lot to shape ethical and romantic life entirely outside the church. Because these questions go deep, they can't be asked too abstractly. They have to be asked and answered in relation to our most intimate experiences of our selves, our institutions and our world.

Poetry seems well adapted to such soundings. In 'Poetry and Religion', the Australian poet Les Murray contends that religions *are* poems which concert our 'daylight and dreaming mind, our / emotions, instinct, breath and native gesture' into that form of thinking which is living itself. It's an interesting position, and one with the attractive corollary that poems are miniature religions – religions, if you like, on imaginative probation. Elsewhere in the poem Murray tells us 'God is the poetry caught in any religion, / caught, not imprisoned'. And the philosopher Martin Heidegger agrees that 'poetic thinking' is nothing less than 'being in the presence of and for the god'.[1] Poetry goes deeper than conceptual thinking, which loses hold of the truth by translating it too quickly into what we think we already know. It is the vehicle of religious discovery. Note, in this connection, the translator's small 'g': God for Heidegger cannot be ossified into a known quantity, but is always to be sought afresh. God is in the questing, not the capture, which makes the poet's search for God the quick, essential element, the very *lifeblood* of religion. Which perhaps explains something of the sheer prophetic conviction with which Emily Brontë apostrophises the truer 'God within my breast' and in 'No Coward Soul Is Mine' declares:

---

[1] See John D. Caputo's edited volume *The Religious*; or Martin Heidegger, *Poetry, Language, Thought*, ed. Albert Hofstadter.

Vain are the thousand creeds
That move men's hearts: unutterably vain;
Worthless as withered weeds,
Or idlest froth amid the boundless main.

Here poetry and private 'spirituality' hold religion to strict account, not vice versa. Still, as Murray insists, a religion attains to the manifest beauty and dignity of *a permanently shared, lived and comprehensive poem*, whereas a poem which is not a religion remains only the flashing possibility of such an impressive thing. A startling passage from Simone Weil's *Gravity and Grace* is relevant in this context:

> Workers need poetry more than bread. They need that
> their life should be a poem. They need some light
>   from eternity.
> Religion alone can give such poetry.
> Deprivation of this poetry explains all forms of
>   demoralization.

All forms of demoralization: if there is anything in what Weil says at all, then the poet's search for God is a very important one indeed.

This volume quests for God within religion – not just Christianity – and beyond it, which, I think, keeps it honest to the pressure and multi-facetedness of the life we now share. Luke Kennard's poem enters a gravel pit. It enters a gravel pit because that's the most desirably unconsecrated place it can imagine in which to discuss the psalms, the point presumably being that religion has to be comprehensively remade, elsewhere, with new materials:

> Because a King is a tyrant or a keyring novelty,
> because a Lord is a landowner with a lifetime peerage.

That certainly resonates with me. But the thirst for God in this poem remains a thirst unslaked even though it's raining so hard that the poet's trouser cuffs brim with 'unholy water' (reminiscences here of Larkin's 'Church Going'). Maybe what we need is an *entirely* new religion. Elizabeth Spires (her name seeming wonderfully to be part of her poem, or registering more negatively that obdurate inheritance which could limit our religious creativity...) dares to imagine 'constructing' one. But it is also possible that poetry could renew our religious traditions from within. Indeed, Andrew Shanks – for my money the most powerful advocate for renewal within the church – suggests in his fine book *What is Truth?* that 'everything, for theology, depends upon its being so far as possible opened up, as a discipline, to the re-energizing power of great, strange, wild poetry – in testimony to the truth which is love'.

All this reminds me of Ted Hughes' *Gaudete*, where an Anglican clergyman called Lumb is spiritually abducted and replaced with a changeling 'who interprets the role of minister in his own way'. One of his parishioners straightforwardly explains that Lumb has a new religion, only women can belong to it, and he makes love to all of them all of the time. That might not be exactly what most new religionists have in mind – though it might be – but it does helpfully emphasise that the poet's quest for God can prove to be a much more than whimsically spiritual or aesthetic thing. And it suggests that it might prove to be so not just elsewhere – in Afghanistan, for example – but here. Shanks argues that the truth beyond dogma to which 'great, strange, wild poetry' opens us could work as an inspiring induction into real moral and political susceptibility and so lead to the positive transformation of the world. It could, and the changes thus demanded might be just as thrillingly or fearsomely extreme as those which Hughes describes.

But who is God? Where is He (or She, because He really might be, as some of the strongest poems suggest here)? The particularly intense suspicion in our time that God isn't in Heaven on His throne suggests to some that He could instead be hiding under any stone. *'Lift the stone and you will find me*; / *Split the wood and I am there'*: Rowan Williams quotes the Gospel of Thomas, but it may be that we've been so shaken out of dogmatic and metaphysical certainty that we've been shaken into a freshly exposed sensitivity to the possibilities of divine immanence in the world. Wallace Stevens, who called for a new intelligence, suggests as much in his poem 'Sunday Morning'. Reading *The Poet's Quest For God* doesn't exactly suggest that 'the world is charged with the grandeur of God' (Hopkins), but perhaps God isn't now to be sought or known in grandeur? At any rate, there's a more subtle hum of presence in this volume. Lois P. Jones tentatively suggests:

> Maybe every blossom is another chance
> at goodness, the purity of a new life,
> a hope to be born into it.

Whereas Carmen Calatayud's poem rests in the simplest, universal blessing of sunlight: 'Everybody's baptised / by the sun and that is all'.

I like 'that is all' and its authoritative, almost religious resistance to metaphysics. In searching for God through the textures of contemporary experience (a pompous way of putting it I know, but I have to indicate somehow that life today is larger, more subtle and more unknown than current stereotyped trends), this volume recalls the legacy of the great German poet, Friedrich Hölderlin. In his preliminary drafts for 'Celebration of Peace', Hölderlin was brave enough to address the 'Conciliator' who is 'no longer believed in'.[2] The miracle, to my mind, of Hölderlin's poem 'Patmos' is its demonstration that just when the certainty is all gone from Christianity and it reappears in its own basic, even prosaic reality, it is as if a light suddenly goes on and it becomes pure, sacred poetry again:

---

2 I quote from Michael Hamburger's reissued translations of 1980.

... and the attentive man
Saw the face of God exactly
When over the mystery of the vine
They sat together at the banqueting hour
And in his great soul, calmly foreknowing,
The Lord pronounced death and the ultimate love, for never
Could he find words enough
To say about kindness, then, and to soothe, when
He saw it, the wrath of the world.
For all things are good. After that he died. Much could
Be said of it. And the friends at the very last
Saw him, the gladdest, looking up triumphant.

In 'Bread and Wine', Hölderlin insists that his subjects are themselves, just bread and wine, and in that sacred; and yet, at the same time, thoroughly deserving the 'serious hymns to the wine-god' they elicit from poets. It is instructive to see poetry here, by simply and demonstrably hallowing that upon which its attention falls, resolving the complex, sometimes absurd theology of transubstantiation: and it intimates an obscure kinship between poetry and religion as agencies of affirmation. Marvelling at the same process, John Biddle writes in this volume, 'I type, there he is / at each key'. Most joyous of all in Hölderlin, this affirmation rebounds upon the humanity which channels it: 'What of the children of God was foretold in the songs of the ancients, / Look, we are it, ourselves; fruit of Hesperia it is!' Though of course the joy didn't last for poor Hölderlin, more of which below.

For now the point is that such restless, syncretic immanentism reverberates like music through *The Poet's Quest For God*. At one point, Philip Gross, looking out into the ordinary world, murmurs across a long line-break, 'If *this* was theology: / .... imagine it'. Indeed, imagine it!

But then presumably part of the meaning of that man-god Christ who said 'I am the way' is that this – this mortal life – *is* theology. And it would seem that poetry might help us recover it.

Of course each reader will have his or her own favourites, but for me David Grubb's affectingly simple image of 'The Blue Cathedral' which 'makes a miracle of being' even if God is not there speaks especially eloquently to the meaning and desire which exceeds common sense but infuses our most personal and precious experience. And the hum of presence in *The Poet's Quest For God* becomes delightfully audible in Sharon Dolin's sonic epiphany of the 6 a.m. thrumming world. We may all have felt something like she describes.

But, in his drafts for 'Celebration of Peace', Hölderlin says, 'A god for a moment only will touch the dwellings of men'. I have suggested this book strings together many such moments like pearls, but otherwise we are – perhaps as we have never been – in the dark. But that's not altogether a gloomy thing, since it's where the mystics have always sought their deity. The truth-disclosing night is a great theme of German Romanticism, in Novalis as well as Hölderlin; but it is anticipated by a great poem of the English (or, rather, Welsh) tradition:

> Dear night! this world's defeat;
> The stop to busy fools; care's check and curb;
> The day of spirits; my soul's calm retreat
>   Which none disturb!
>   Christ's progress, and His prayer time;
>   The hours to which high heaven doth chime.
>
>   God's silent, searching flight:
> When my Lord's head is filled with dew, and all
> His locks are wet with the clear drops of night;
>   His still, soft call;
>   His knocking time; the soul's dumb watch,
>   When spirits their fair kindred catch.

God can rarely have been so deliciously present in a poem as in this one. Henry Vaughan's 'The Night' presents a sacred reservation from all the mad, destructive busyness of the daylight world which I take it many of us will recognise. Vaughan's is a night so rich in truth you can almost reach out and touch the hair of God, savouring its dew-sculpted coldness, even while fair spirits loop, embrace and tumble in silent catherine wheels around you...

Like Vaughan, the poets in this volume move sometimes to switch out the lights. 'Every True Religion is Bound to Fail', as Charles Bernstein's poem has it, since it is merely a human artefact; it has to give way to God. What's needed is what Wordsworth nominates 'wise passiveness' ('Expostulation and Reply'), which in these pages Karen Winterburn more starkly calls 'surrender'. And indeed if God is truly transcendent, only a complete relinquishing of the self and its faculties will do. For, as Hilary Davies writes:

> How does the ear prepare
> For what it does not even know
> It cannot hear?

If God resides in darkness, then poetry can only approach him by itself going dark and into the dark, and this will be a fearful as well as a beautiful thing.

We have to take our chance with D. H. Lawrence, who reaches deep into the textured darkness of death in 'Bavarian Gentians'. It's a darkness thickened, too, with moral uncertainty, with questionable, 'Plutonic' desires: a darkness of our own selves as well as what's beyond us. It's tempting of course to lighten this immediately! But even if we do the darkness remains. If we're to come to grips with it, it has to become 'darkness visible' (Milton); it will have to be illumined by some paradoxically dark light, just such as Lawrence holds up before him 'in the blue, forked torch' of his gentian.

Any search for God has to negotiate the big, dark obstacles of evil and pain, which would seem to set serious limits to God's power or goodness, if not to rule out His existence altogether. The great wrestle with this in modern poetry is Ted Hughes' explosive *Crow*. And, forty some years after first publication, the tracks of *Crow* still show up in *The Poet's Quest For God*. Benno Barnard's 'Agnostic Evensong' imagines 'a murder of crows' celebrating 'their vespers of objection'. And April Bulmer writes:

> Oh to be a Sister,
> to bear the cross,
> the weight of His burden.
>
> Instead, something this way comes:
> a crow, his wing tipped in blood.

These lines recognise that Crow emerges from *Macbeth*, and thus from the heart of the English literary tradition. In Hughes, Crow explicitly takes upon himself all the darkness of evil and pain. This gives those forces their ultimate status (and what else in our experience is more ultimate?) which more feel-good representations of God evade. Crow represents the darkness in and of God, which is why he bites a bit off God's body in the poem 'Crow Communes'. He embodies the energy of evil, but also its suffering. Crow shivers with the horror of creation, which in his own being he nonetheless expresses, 'every feather the fossil of a murder' ('Crow Alights', 'Crow's Nerve Fails').

In Hughes' black book, the agonies of human sexuality come down to Crow attempting to pronounce the word 'love' at God's direction. In fact, they issue from his third such miserable attempt. The first time he tries a great white shark flops out of his beak, 'discovering its own depth' ('Crow's First Lesson'). The darkness to which Hughes grants such unforgettable form is the darkness earlier articulated by Blake:

> The roaring of lions, the howling of wolves, the raging of the stormy sea, and the destructive sword, are portions of eternity too great for the eye of man. (*The Marriage of Heaven and Hell*)

It is confronted in *The Poet's Quest For God* when William Oxley writes of 'the ultimate good in a world where there is / no, yes, no ultimate good', and when Philip Fried in 'Quantum Genesis' says with fierce, fiercely judgemental comedy:

> His perfection
> is great and unstable and His shame
> perfect and vast.

There is no alternative to coping with this darkness. In present conditions, as Geoffrey Hill insists in 'Genesis', 'There is no bloodless myth will hold'.

Hölderlin suggests in 'Patmos' that where danger is there also grows what saves. Maybe, but the risks are dreadful. Hölderlin went mad. In Jericho Brown's seethingly reticent 'Prayer of the Backhanded', it's hard to know whether the son's intercession for his abusive father is saintly and heroic or a pitiful reverberation of the original abuse – and it's just as hard to separate the abusive father from the God (if God there be) who one way or another will defeat and kill us all, or at least stand by and watch. In 'Disillusion', Grahame Davies attempts to face all this and go on trying:

> And now, knowing this,
> expecting nothing,
> wanting nothing,
> fearing nothing,
> to trust, to give, to love.

It's no less of a heroic creed for being what we all have to do, all of the time.

And yet – those epiphanies, those spots of time, given in the following pages and discussed above continue, sometimes unpredictably, to interrupt the darkness. As Herbert writes in 'The Flower', 'Grief melts away / Like snow in May, / As if there were no such cold thing'. It really does, except when it doesn't, and sometimes it melts into a happiness as positive as that which Clea Roberts records:

> There is a child at my bedside
> stroking my cheek – I did not ask
> for this blessing.

Part of the beauty of such moments is that they are more than we deserve. Because, as *Crow* recognises, if we're victims, we are also perpetrators, all of us guilty as sin. One of the most impressive and precious things in this book, I think, is Brigit Pegeen Kelly's beautiful poem about a decapitated goat's head singing in a tree. The goat had belonged to and been loved by a girl. She sang him songs, she brushed his coat. She dreamed about him, and she dreamed that her dreams made him grow. The boys hack off the goat's head for fun. It's harder than expected. They string it up in a tree. Others dispose of it, in order to spare the girl distress. They buy her another goat. But the goat's head sings. It sings from the moment it is severed from its neck; it sings to the boys who behead it.

> Not a cruel song, no, no, not cruel at all. This song
> Is sweet. It is sweet. The heart dies of this sweetness.

'Listen', the poem begins.

THE POET'S QUEST FOR GOD

M.J. ABELL

BLESSED IS THE WOMAN
Adaptation of a passage from Ecclesiasticus

Blessed is the woman
who goes after Wisdom like a tracker
and stays on Her trail. Blessed is she
who looks in Wisdom's windows
and listens at Her door.
Blessed is she who camps her tent
near Wisdom's house, fastening tent pegs
to Her wall, creating her sacred space.
That woman is sheltered
under Wisdom's branches, protected
under Her covering from the heat. She rests
in Wisdom's own radiance.
Blessed, blessed that woman.

SHANTA ACHARYA

I DO NOT KNOW

After Shaikh Fakhruddin Ebrahim Hammedani

Are you the universe and all existence,
        in all things and beyond all things?
I do not know...

Are you the breath that keeps me alive
        or the moments that take my breath away?
I do not know...

Are you the slayer or the slain, both or neither,
I do not know...

Why does your omnipotence tolerate
        so much injustice in this world?
I do not know...

Are you immanent or transcendent,
        unknowable or the One reaching out to us?
I do not know...

Do you pour suffering on us
        to mould us towards your purpose?
I do not know...

When I find doubt reigning supreme in my heart,
        is that also your way?
I do not know...

Why do you hide from your creation?
I do not know...

I thought I had an understanding with you
        but you took it away years ago.

Did you replace it with a superior covenant
        or simply renege on our contract?
I do not know...

If I cannot find you in my heart,
        in living creatures, in the eyes of my enemies;
where can I go looking for you,
        let me know for I am tired and bewildered.
I do not know...

If I cannot see your beauty, recognise
        your magnificence, what hope is there for me?

You taught me to find nothing in my heart
        except the compassion of your Love
And yet I do not know...

When will I be released from this separation;
        where do I end, and you begin?
I do not know...

PAUL ADRIAN

SISTINE CHAPEL, 1510

68ft up, Michelangelo
lies nose to nose with the Lord, still wet.
Adam's finger remains to be painted.
The scaffolding he built himself, from wood,
a tower tall enough to grasp the scale
of falling short, and fill the span
with heavens.
                        Look closely at the pigments.
Sky blue. Olive green. Resurrection yellow.
The artist exercising his palette.
The variation in the shades (of red
for example – rose petal, apple, blood)
betrays some process of selection, the pale
gap between *chosen* and *also ran*.
In time, he will begin *The Last Judgement*.

PATIENCE AGBABI

I GO BACK TO MAY 1967
After Sharon Olds

I see them standing outside their family compounds,
I see my father wearing a white agbadan and
crocodile shoes, instructing his driver by the
spiked iron gate of their complex, he is just
twenty-four but already a big man in Lagos. It is
rainy season, the air heavy with his looming proposal. I
see my mother walking barefoot on the red dust road to her
village, a calabash on her head, wearing her only cloth and
crucifix, she has just fetched water from the well.
They have not yet met, today they will be married.
My father will arrive in his Cadillac to
translate her into his bride, adorned with gold.
I want to approach them and say Stop,
I am begging you – you are not a bad woman,
he is not a good man, he is going to put you on trial
like Job: you will bear him a daughter, and later a son,
and each time he will say his people have turned against you
because you are from a small village and not educated,
each baby must be removed by force from your breast
(but he will secretly place us in care of my aunt
to attend the best schools in the country)
and you will draw the sign of the cross on our heads,
your womb will cry out but you will not disgrace him
for you promised to honour and obey; in time, he will claim
he wants a new wife, believes in one man one wife
and wants divorce, will send you back to your village
barefoot and bareheaded with barely a cloth to cover
the belly that bore him two children; then order you back
like a house-girl to manage the house and the wedding feast
for his beautiful new wife from a good family

who resembles you, because it is I, your daughter,
standing before you, young, adorned with gold;
and only when you say, Oga, please I beg you,
do not treat your new wife the way you have treated me,
will he reveal his deception to test your faith
in him and your love of the Lord Jesus Christ. I want to
approach them, there in the late May heat and say it,
her hungry pretty face turning towards me
slow motion with the weight of the calabash,
his arrogant handsome face turning towards me
slowly with the precious weight on his mind.
But I do not say it. I want to live my life. I
take them up like Shango and Oshun
mahogany dolls and rub them together
at the hips, wood on wood, as if to
make fire from them, and I say
do what is God's will and I will bear witness.

NEIL AITKEN

TRAVELING THROUGH THE PRAIRIES, I THINK OF MY FATHER'S VOICE

How we must have seemed like twins over the phone,
my father speaking with my voice, I speaking with his.
Some strange accident of genetics or the unchecked influence

of mockingbirds and mimeographs. I have heard two trains sound
almost alike till they passed, like the one last night bending westward,
the other slowing to a halt, the earth shuddering in the dark between

while the stars held their place overhead, a thousand points of tin and fire.
Had it been day, I might have seen to the far faded edge of nowhere
or whatever town lies wakeless there. Here, the wind sounds the same

blown from any direction, full of dust, pollen, the deep toll of church bells
rung for mass, weddings, deaths. Coming through on the straight road,
the land seems especially bare this year, although the fields are still green

with new stalks of wheat, rye, canola. Someone has been taking down
the grain elevators one by one, striking their weathered wooden frames
from the skyline, leaving only small metal bins. The way the disease

took him by degrees, the body jettisoning what it could: his arms and legs,
his grin, his laugh, his voice. In the end, only his eyes – their steel doors
opening and closing while the storm rattled within – and his breath,

the body's voice, repeating the only name it knew sigh after sigh,
a lullaby sung to a restless child on a heaving deck, a hush we only learn
in the quiet dark long after the boat has gone and the waves have ceased.

ANTONIA ALEXANDRA

THE BELIEVER

I have faith in the darkness
that surrounds me –
in the holy unspoken prayer
the unborn child
the photograph coming to light

So small am I in my inertia
like Nothing hurtling through
the eternal chasm of my loneliness
And, yet, only out of the depths
am I able to climb deeper into That
which holds me suspended
in the knowable Unknown

I do not know if am
sinking or rising star
morning or evening
What does it matter?
I just keep climbing
out of myself
out of that dark hole
I have dug once too often

into the Holiness
into the Holiness

KAZIM ALI

DOOR BETWEEN YOU

In the cabin next to yours you hear voices
Keeping you awake in the lumbering night
What slumber slackens lack will open
He is tapping the wall between you
Going on and on about how we are all creatures of energy and light
'Reachers' you think is good common sense
But did he really just say 'injuries of light?'

RICHARD ALI

FLOWER IN THE SUN
for Master Jalaludin R

Eyes above cobwebs, I find space beyond reason
One foot flat while the other traces the curling notes
Of a gwogie, irregular like leaves of breeze blown palms;
Care-fetters forgotten, my torso turns through a slow full arc

The One is sun, circles of energy, an endless garden where
Sphere music sustains my every whirl as a flower-top
Spinning on a force field. Illumined by It, my eyes find
Beneath myriad ways a common trail running.

I dance in my white sheet and all the Prophets come
To watch me blossoming in the garden, purifying my will;
Seven djinns come to test me, demanding the kalimat shahada
I do not stop, I reply; there is, one God, there is. Just One God.

MAUREEN ALSOP

ALCOVE

Snow lacerates the valley. Meaning there is no disrespect
for transition – flakes puncturing the dry edge of your bootstep. This
reminds me. Your breath's stitchery, gray
needle in unclenched motion, translucent
      chlorine-scented hospital linoleum where
itinerants do not regret a plasticized sensibility. O, synthetic semi-silver –
the beholden rub no wound. Meanwhile
                           I have no identity
    and do not remember if remembering
is the response required for this particular century. Coins
    spill my pocketbook as constellation, the practical application
of language – it made of me   a success
    for I can roam the dark with grave bravado. But do I really believe
this room as a prairie of indefinite beginnings? I judge
the striation's trail as a casket of tiny bellflower blossoms.

FRED ANDRLE

YOU ALWAYS HAVE AN ANSWER

When I say:
I think God visited me in a dream last night.
You say: So what was it you ate for dinner?
When I say:
I think that God may have a perfect love for you and me.
You say: Wishful thinking.
When I say:
My grandfather spoke to me from heaven.
You say: That was your brain chemistry talking.
And when I say:
Maybe, just maybe, we'll have life eternal.
You say: Where's your evidence?
I've heard your answers for so long now
I think they must come from a broken heart
come sit with me for a while
let us put aside all these questions, these opinions.
Maybe infinite love will touch us
maybe in silence He will cherish us
maybe there will be no more need for
my doubt, your certitude, our terrible loss.

MARIA APICHELLA

JAR

We live life to life,
Like a cloud
Of tadpoles swirling
In an invisible jar.

God is lidless
Filled with drinkable rain,
The shape and dimension
Of our days. I sense this.
You don't. Even so,
We move in the same water
Searching our mouth-like brains
For something deep to grow in.

Give me patience
Contain me,
I am swarming.

ROBERT ARCHAMBEAU

HIERATIC PERSPECTIVE

I went into the cathedral that was for me alone,
where the guide who was also for me alone,

and of me alone, spoke to me alone
of the niche-bound altarpiece

that mapped my spirit out for me.
He said:

'God's holy fire, sure, is in these
panels, damaged, gold, and glorious,

perched in the cathedral only you
have ever stepped in

(you and I are here – right! –
but you and I are one, if even that).

So look what's there, on the altarpiece,
its images, Italo-Byzantine,

in that gold-on-gold terrarium, the angel ant-farm
of that flattened space. A clustering of haloed heads,

consecrate, and hallowed, and decayed.
Front and centre, at six-foot-eight,

almost the full height of the panel, there:
blue-robed and bulky: your libido,

the fine-drawn bright bits
chipped away – a blue tempera

never lasts. We cannot
tell the gender, anymore, if it were ever manifest

(sources are vague, and disagree, and written
by monks – what would they know?). Faceless,

it keeps the object of desire there,
dandled on its knee – she's smudged-up

by the candle smoke, a little limb is left, you see, a little
pink-fleshed arm, a haunch, and something of a mouth,

quite cruel.
The tiny putti dancing at her feet are appetites,

so many I've often asked myself
'was there an explosion at the cherub factory?'

And kneeling, off to either side: the patrons. If they stood
they wouldn't reach that central figure's knees. And then behind:

their clustered heads a mass of dazzled haloed light,
the patron saints of work, and reputation,

of jokes and reefer, drink, and hanging out, the patron saint
of art. What are they? Two-foot three? A choir

to sing and cry for you. To look upward
at that high-placed panel that was never painted,

or (here sources disagree)
we've lost'.

I went, again, into the cathedral that was for me alone,
where the guide who was also for me alone,

who was also me, alone,
and I looked away, to where curled smoke

sleep-walked and grew tall and taller
above the altar,

wove ropes around itself, and disappeared.

RAE ARMANTROUT

BELIEVING

1

When did you first learn
that the bursts

of color and sound
were intended for you?

When did you unlearn this?

2

Believing yourself
to have a secret identity
can be a sign
of madness.

On the other hand,
the lack
of a secret identity
can lead to depression.
Many have found it useful
to lie down
as men
believing themselves
to be little girls

or as girls
believing themselves
to be mermaids
stranded
in their own bodies.

DAVID BAKER

MERCY

Small flames afloat in blue duskfall, beneath trees
anonymous and hooded, the solemn tress — by ones
and twos and threes we go down to the water's level edge
with our candles cupped and melted into little pie-tins
to set our newest loss free. Everyone is here.

Everyone is wholly quiet in the river's hush and appropriate dark.
The tenuous fires slip from our palms and seem to settle
in the stilling water, but then float, ever so slowly,
in a loose string like a necklace's pearls spilled,
down the river barely as wide as a dusty road.

No one is singing, and no one leaves — we stand back
beneath the grieving trees on both banks, bowed but watching,
as our tiny boats pass like a long history of moons
reflected, or like notes in an elder's hymn, or like us,
death after death, around the far, awakening bend.

JENNIFER BARBER

TO BREAK IT OPEN,

to make
the orange lantern
of the flower
open, to wash
my hands in its light.

Last bees in the yard,
the drowsy leaves

leaking their slow
red and gold.

One of the sages
in the book
I read and misplaced

said there was no time
to finish the harvest,

the day short,
the night
long – the Master near.

RACHEL BARENBLAT

EL SHADDAI (NURSING POEM)

Was God overwhelmed
when Her milk first came in

roused by our thin cries
for compassion?

She'd birthed creation
from amoebas to galaxies

but did She expect to see
Her own changeability

mirrored behind our eyes?
Nothing could have prepared Her

for the shift from singularity
to multiplicity.

And the blank-faced angels
offered their constant praise

without understanding Her joy
or the depth of Her fear.

SEBASTIAN BARKER

TALKING SYMBOLS

Translate, O flowers, into verse
To rid me of the doubter's curse.
Your open faces say to me
Christ's love is God's true poetry.
The sun's his golden fountain pen
You open to in gardens when
You watch him writing on the floor
Uncountable magnitudes of more.
Flowers! The intellect vanishes
Into the intelligence he banishes.
All that's left is talking symbols
Extolling God as godless dwindles.

BENNO BARNARD

AGNOSTIC EVENSONG
Saint Davids, Wales

In a valley full of psalms and nightingales,
he lay beside a river on the bank of a cathedral
reading the cotton-thread clouds on a violet evening.

Flowering valerian everywhere. Bible-blithe people
bowed their heads like blades of grass and the bells
chimed his personal invitation – it was a *huis clos*

of grace and as the wind erased the writing
of those clouds, he lay there by that water and was
oh so joyous. Death was there as well: a murder

of crows celebrated their vespers of objection,
while the heron-like priest regurgitated a formidable
centuries-old sentence, that every man is a piece

of the Continent etc. Then the choir filled the dish
that seemed to serve him up: the dragonflies
hung in the air, as if planning to settle him...

Calm down, molecules! You're a clod of Europe,
let me embrace you before you wash away and drown,
he thought, confused. But dozed off on valerian.

He lay in that valley listening to the canon for choir
and crows, the holy words, the diaphanous hovering;
and from the bells above him time rained down.

Translated by David Colmer

MICHAEL BARTHOLOMEW-BIGGS

INCARNATION

You burst into our conversation
like the sudden stranger
striding through a bar room.
You split our boasting, wooing, whining
with a silence measured
by the rolling tick-tock
of a toppled empty glass;
the drop of dominoes
dribbling off a table;
the ripple of a pack of cards
self-shuffling while escaping
from a dealer's grip.

Before the raising of a voice
you cut the moment short
and quit the floor, to let
the laughter and the bartering
choose to start again.
The swing doors spread and shut
behind your unprotected back
as if to beckon any
who might dare to follow,
empty-handed and alone,
and face you in the dark
beyond the disused stable.

MICAH BATEMAN

O AS ZERO SUM (A PSALM)

End this, Lord. I said I said no.
You saw the O of my mouth
Surrounding the vowel,

Slurred fret of morning time in the slow stirring
Of my cereal O's.
See the O as spoon, Lord,

O as rounded spade –
Dig and feed Lord I open the O for sustenance
But nothing.

Have you seen how we advertise zeroness?
O is for zero calories.
O is for pitiful Onan.

O is the round of the long canal of the body
Down which zeroness flows and empties,
Lord it's like this,

We must get the jackal, chicken, and corn
Across the river. The river flows
But none will enter

Alive. Jackal takes chicken; chicken, corn.
What is left but entropy? River wins.
The boat scurries its course, emptied.

My father's father enters the boat.
My mother's mother enters the boat.
The boat is a cavity that cannot enclose

One tiny morsel. O energy.
This letter, Lord help us.
How can one graph a sound so empty?

Take a photo of the choir and trace the mouths.
I said no, I did. I said: Mandible,
No, I won't let you down.

SHAINDEL BEERS

FROM THIRTEEN WAYS OF LOOKING AT A PELICAN

For centuries it was believed that the pelican
was an allegory for Christ. That the young
would begin with their new, sharp beaks,

to wound their parents, drawing their blood,
and the parents, in their anger, would smite them.
After three days of mourning the mother (some

accounts say the father) would open its breast,
and the hot drops of blood would bring the young
back to life. This allegory was to teach of Christ's

love. His sacrifice on the cross. Bartholomaeus
Anglicus wrote in the 13th Century, *The pelican
loveth too much her children*. The same way

I was taught that Adam's sin was uxoriousness.
But I was taught that we could never love Christ
too much, that we were to devote our lives to Him.

Instead, I choose the mountains, the rivers.
They open their hearts to us every day
no matter how we wound them.

MICHAEL S. BEGNAL

THE EWES AT IMBOLC

I appear in the animal world
this time
blood and drums,
another body to be burned

in golden flame
the sun radiant afire –
an ever-fine woman
leads us to everlasting day

stanzas burned up in flames,
everything good we have
could easily be lost
in the conflagration

ascertain, via
the sense of our animal body
transitory birth
or births?

the ewes heaving with lambs,
the ewes lactating them
on higher ground,
the lambs lying down

in the melting snow
on the hills, spattered among rocks
already the grasses coming up,
the lambs lie down

wild ewes and lambs,
cats too, a coming spring
on tufts of new grass
green and soft like skin

some animals we have been,
some animals we may still be,
their sprawling selves by the fire,
the elegant taking of prey

MARGO BERDESHEVSKY

DUSK

This is the place. No chairs.
A woman who is choosing
has sent a petal from her bloom
of conscious closing.

The woman who is choosing when
— scratches vellum. The rook stands.
The woman in the nest of
the phoenix hovers nearer
her edge like that brood of birthing

opal-throated pigeons in an empty
flower trough,
thirsty, one stair above my sill,
breaking their shells one by

one. She repeats
my words
from dusk in a jungle where
medicine leaned small against thorn trees.
Each poison growing in a forest

lives beside its antidote, we said.
I am still eager, I said.
Or the scent of hyacinth.
The woman remembering, who is

choosing when to die will
curl before leaves have blood-burned September.
Surrender by starvation,
she doesn't name her illness

only how many days.
Three more. The woman
in worn white cotton washed us in a tide pool,
brewed petals, shouted under

egrets at the edge of rain. Bon voyage to me & love
life as you live it she scribbles blue before her breath
ends a night and a day and the broken slant
dawn.

The woman who was choosing when to die.
Too young to be skeletal, skin taken wing.
Bone no longer needed. Dove.
Fire-eyed. Distant. Opal.

The root does not care
where her water comes from.
Here is another thirsty body.
Broken into morning.

CHARLES BERNSTEIN

EVERY TRUE RELIGION IS BOUND TO FAIL

Only the Divine truth reveals itself
In lies, smarter truths Disguise themselves as
Fundament or wise. On the way from dusk
To Dark, slip to slap, pitch to black, a Haze
Cries sudden slow, searing sworn, Betrays de-
Lay's sullied song. Ev'ry true monument
Lays in shards, layered with tongues. The trip to
Caution foments Alarm, as lulled to
Passion, Action never reverses Wrong –
No Certainty ever could Cancel right.

Tried syrup for a while, round of sweetness
For ton of Tears. Fault of fellows, rusty
Melons that mock the girls and make us dry.
Mock the curls and make men sigh.

ASHOK BERY

THE FIRE SERMON

I have heard that on one occasion the Blessed One was dwelling at Gaya,
at Gaya's Head, together with a thousand bhikkhus. There he addressed the monks.
The Adittapariyaya Sutta

'Everything's on fire', he said,
'The tongue and the mind, the eye and the ear –
Can you hear them
Crackling with desire,
With hatred and anger and fear,
With the flames of birth and death?
Let them all go,
Let them float off on your breath,
The way the Ganga takes the dead.'
I can never let go
Of anything: love gone cold,
Old jiffy bags, piles of recipes clipped from the Sundays,
Pencil stubs too small to hold,
The *TLSs* I shoved in a cupboard
Or left to gather dust beneath the bed –
A hopeful tick against so many books
Which, one day,
I will never have read.

JOAN BIDDLE

GOD IN ST. PAUL DE VENCE

The sky is swollen,
the fields sprout his face.

I type, there he is
at each key.

I walk upstairs, he sits
in my chair and waits.

But I've already sugared
and salted the sheets,

climbed out the window
to feel the rain.

MALACHI BLACK

QUARANTINE

Lauds

Somehow I am sturdier, more shore
than sea-spray as I thicken through
the bedroom door. I gleam of sickness.
You give me morning, Lord, as you
give earthquake to all architecture.
I can forget.
                        You put that sugar
in the melon's breath, and it is wet
with what you are. (I, too, ferment.)
You rub the hum and simple warmth
of summer from afar into the hips
of insects and of everything.
I can forget.
                        And like the sea,
one more machine without a memory,
I don't believe that you made me.

Prime

I don't believe that you made me
into this tremolo of hands,
this fever, this flat-footed dance
of tendons and the drapery

of skin along a skeleton.
I am that I am: a brittle
ribcage and the hummingbird
of breath that flickers in it.

Incrementally, I stand:
in me are eons and the cramp
of endless ancestry.

Sun is in the leaves again.
I think I see you in the wind
but then I think I see the wind.

Terce

But then I think I see the wind
as an intention, pressing us
with weather. All the pieces
of the air you've put together
somehow know just how to hold
the rain. They somehow know

to funnel and unfold, to swerve
the snow, to rake the beaches
and to slope the arcing seagull's wings.
As wind inside a shell: they know
you in themselves. I'll find you out;
I can know you as a hint in things.

I do. And through the window
I have known you as an opening.

Sext

I have known you as an opening
of curtains as a light blurts through
the sky. But this is afternoon
and afternoon is not the time

to hunt you with the hot globe
of a human eye. So I fluster
like a crooked broom in rounds
within the living room, and try
to lift an ear to you. I try.

I cut myself into a cave for you.
To be a trilling blindness
in the infinite vibration
of your murmuring July,
I cut myself into a cave for you.

None

I cut myself into a cave for you,
but you are quiet. You are shy:

an only child, you still hide
from blame and invitations

and you constantly deny
all suitors. I will not be

defied: *you* are the tongue
I plunge into this begging

razorblade so brightened
by my spiderweb of blood,

you are the one: you are
the venom in the serpent

I have tried not to become,
my Lord. You are the one.

Vespers

My Lord, you are the one:
your breath has blown away
     the visionary sun
and now suffocates the skyline
     with a dusk. If only once,
I wish that you could shudder
with my pulse,   double over
and convulse   on the stitches
in the skin that I slash wishes in.
     But, Lord, you are the gulf
between the hoped-for
        and the happening:
You've won.   So what is left for me
when what is left for me has come?

Compline

when what is left for me has come:
when what is left has left its wing
in something slumped against a door:
when what is left for me has come
to nothing ever after and before
this kingdom come to nothing:
when what has come is nothing more
than what was left and what was left
is nothing more than what has come
to nothing ever after and before:
if what is left is what is meant
for me and what is meant for me
is nothing come to nothing come
to this kingdom come to nothing:

Nocturne

To This Kingdom Come to Nothing:

I have itemized the night. I have held
within the livid tissue of my mouth
every particle of light and even now
I am a maze of radiation. I have felt
in each of my one hundred trillion cells
the rapturous, proud swell of darkling sounds
whose undulations break a body down
to sprays of elemental matter. As well
I have obtained a straightforward account
of the forces and conditions that propelled
the universe to burst from nothing else
and I can tell of every trembling genesis.

There is no end,

                    What Has Come
                              Will Come Again

Vigils

There is no end: what has come will come again
will come again: and then distend: and then
and then: and then again: there is no end

to origin and and: there is again
and born again: there is the forming and:
the midnight curling into morning and

the glory and again: there is no end:
there is the blessing in an and and an again:
the limitlessly yessing of began

begins incessantly again: and then
the infinite undressing of all when
there is the lifting everything again

the glowing endlessness and then
the floating endlessly again

Matins

The floating endlessly again:
the glowing and the growing back
again as I am as I can and I can stand.
I understand.
           Though I am fashioned
in the haggard image of a man,
I am an atom of the aperture.

I am as a nerve inside a gland.

I understand. Though I am fashioned
as I am, I am a perch for the eternal
and a purse for what it lends.
I understand.
           Though flakes of fire
overwhelm the fallen snow, though ice
caps melt, though oceans freeze or overflow,
somehow I am sturdier, more sure.

JANE BLANCHARD

NAVIGATION

As I cruise along
without a care in the world,
I am tempted to believe
that all is smooth sailing
since the sky is mostly clear
and the sea is fairly calm
for a masterful pilot
such as myself.

But then a storm breaks
with thunder and lightning
and the rain pours down
and the wind blows hard
while the waves crash
over the sides of the skiff
that I vainly try to steer
towards safety.

Once again I must resist
the siren call of self-control,
not by strapping myself
to the mast of my vessel,
but by throwing myself
on the mercy of one
who needs no boat
to cross the water.

YVONNE BLOMER

NIMBUS NOON

Noon in the church of the tomb of Christ
noon and the padre's voice
rises to meet the mid-day sun

Noon in the tree tops   in the nettles and pines
noon and the voice of one   Raven   rises
        to cast out stars   left from last night's dreams
to scare belief   but for belief in this unkindness

Noon   nimbus   haloed   noon
and the birth of this what will come –
one black-eyed baby – magnetic mercurial

hot

hot as spears   as charged particles   life
        from this   secular   su(o)n

MURRAY BODO

SILENCE

Could God be silence, after all
After all the words, rituals
Proclamations, incantations?
After the hymns and processions
After tears and lamentations,
Could silence be the answer?

Silence loud with divinity
No words, no thoughts, no images
Could silence be the God of prayer

As when, silent, he wrote in sand
And she – smelling his feet – heard?

MICHELLE BOISSEAU

I LOVE A PARADE

She knows a spoonful of religion.
It's very shiny. Over the dunes,
along the ocean, she steadies it

at the end of her hand. Like ribbons
wandering behind her, her children
follow their own trembling spoons. Careless

grasses congregate in the sand. Smirk
of surf, cough of gull, I must confess
I'm not trying that hard to love her.

STEPHANIE BOLSTER

VESPERS

Plum brandy, *entre chien et loup*, uppermost
white pine, bequeath.

Once the choir in King's College reached such a note together
you believed in an elsewhere other
than the inside of your head.

She's down now, eyes shut, her breathing slow,
her feet warm under the alphabet quilt she wanted
when the blinds slid together against the light.

From much farther out than here
the city illumines the purplish, reddish
conflagration of jazz, espresso
after dinner, sweat
within the elbow.

Television in the back neighbours' basement window,
now as in winter. You never
recognise that house from the front.

Is home the street you live on or the house
or the room or the word or the first.
The place you long for just before you leave.

JEMMA BORG

TO HOPKINS' GOD

I do still think of you but the feeling is lean.
      The world can't gather its grandeur and share
things with me, and I can't feel my bare being
      or the spring or the westward-heading sun.
The ghosts of those who toiled with faith walk
      their silence through the walls and into the night.
I used to think as they did, but that dream left nothing
      for this world. I'll go to where the soil is charged,
in the east. There, where the light broods, the world
      is becoming *almost* and then actually *becoming*.
I'll wake to the rain and my lover's back, and remember
      a love lower than the sky. It is a work of will,
but the world still shines: I see the bright-fantastic.
      You, however, have folded your wings, and decline.

TODD BOSS

A BLESSING

May the good
Lord grant you
a little pride,

since of Creation
He Himself was
more than a little

satisfied. And
while He's at it
may He cede

some greed,
from Heaven
where His gold is

guaranteed.
And envy too
upon ye pour,

He who will not
suffer any other
gods before.

And wrath! — oh,
yes, God grant
you wrath;

Noah knows
how much
God hath.

A glutton for
praise, may He
see and raise ye

(if He can admit
He's got 'ny)
gluttony.

And I protest:
if all men must
steer clear of lust,

how come He
carved Eve such
a curvy bust?

It isn't just.
Seven flames
for the moth;

the Arsonist on
His arse, too lazy
to snuff them out,

the sloth.

PENNY BOXALL

ST. GILES, FROM A WINDOW

Thursday, and they're ringing in the night —
the birdsong tenor of the bells
   is looped like a complex knot.
They're practising for when it counts.
   The blossoms shake their little
heads but mean assent. They are light
   as ash, and do not last as long.
Spring is compacted, thick and green.

The church is a stolid old stone
in four lanes of noise, unmoved.
   In old prints this is a wilderness,
the packhorses tramping the last
   weary half-mile to the gates.
This used to be a walk, the church its end.
   When I open my window I am closer
to all of it, I let it all in.
 I never see the weddings, but I hear
   their effect. The bells shake
fit to burst, each one shouting out
   so that traffic almost stops. Unseen,
inside, it's finished, and the bells begin again.
   Only the timing changes,
the high bells lagging, clamouring against
   that heavy bass-note which is always right:

though each one has to think that it
   will sound out loudest, count the most.
Each one has to think it, or the whole
   thing will crumble like wet cake. *And oh,*
but this time is the best time, this time is the best.

ASA BOXER

THE SNAKE AND THE LAMB

The snake opened up like a tunnel to the womb.
The lamb slid in. The snake clamped down.
And now the snake seems pregnant with the lamb.
And now the lamb sleeps in the skin of a snake.

At first he felt a tickle by his hind-leg, then a brush
past his shank, a caress across the chest, a nudge
past the ears like a mothering tongue. Then a squeeze
growing tighter, like the love of ten-thousand wombs.

Though the lamb kicked for air, the snake held fast,
for the love of a snake holds tighter than life.
The world went black. The lamb fell limp.
The snake then bound and bagged his prey.

And now, the reptile troubles over each woolly bite;
he must stomach every ingredient of lamb,
the tough and the tender, the flesh and the fat.
Every last cell of snake must come to the table.

Every last scale must welcome the lamb.
In their dreams they are one where awake they struggled.
The lamb must sleep to quiet the snake.
The snake must sleep to swallow the lamb.

DAVID BRIGGS

FLORENTINE

To the educated medieval mind
time maintained merely
the illusion of linearity;

such that those moments painted on commission
by Leonardo, Botticelli or Titian
when the Great Lummox poked his Roman

nose into the human cataclysm,
only *seem* to be occurring sequentially
when they all take place simultaneously

and forever, Amen,
in some cosmically baffling 'Now' or 'Then'.
Thus, the cloistered monk of St. Marco

would commission Fra Angelico
to adorn the walls of his cell
with a crucifixion or harrowing of hell

showing his preferred canonical superstar
(typically, Cosmas, Dominic or Anthony of Padua)
in anachronistic attendance. Hence, too, the

disdain of the Florentine waiter
for an impatient English diner
under the sunshade of his trattoria.

TRACI BRIMHALL

HYSTERIA: A REQUIEM

Kyrie

After the plague
      we put away our lamentation,
                    our children's cradles,
    and dance with all the required ecstasy.

The monks follow us with brooms, barefoot.
          The doctors in the next room
                   heal each other.

    A woman in a mask leads the midwife
by a leash through the rooms.
                Behind her hood she warns,
A nation has ended, but the world continues,
          jubilant and unclean.

Outside, spring continues without us.
      We loved a god we didn't believe in,
    and believed in a god we didn't love,
         but neither let our children live.

Through cracks in the boarded windows, I see broken rocking
horses in the streets. I hear nothing. Nothing. Not even the
wind. I want to go through the houses and search for the living,
but I am bound to the known. A sore rises on my scalp. I tell no
one. The test of faith is not death, but fear.

Dies Irae

No one wants to remember
        how we found bodies in trees and left them
    unburied in the sky.

On ruined carpets we wallow with pomegranates and sweet wine.
    We want to forget the wayfarer we hung
        when he asked for food.

                            The truffles and caviar are ours.
        And the figs.   The rosemary butter and ginger tea.
            The killdeer singing in the wet grass.

We aren't good with memories, but we are serious
            about pleasure.
    About arias and cinnamon.
                    Harps and honey.

_____

I met my love at the gallows where his father taught him to tie
a noose. He lashed his wrists to mine. We tried to burn every
cathedral in the country. Each time the stones bewildered us, so
we traveled to the forest of the damned to baptize the trees. We
wanted to become shadowless, like the sea, but the darkness that
followed us shared our names.

Offertory

The feral cats cry in estrous
        followed by nurses with a cautious hope.

    They unearth the placentas under the stairs,
        but the kittens are born

bathed in flame.
Their mothers eat their fevers
as we intone our cold hallelujahs.

We want to believe laughter will return to us.
We make our hearts
hosts for immortal breath.
Mortify our flesh,
we plead
to the whips in our hands.

The bread does not promise to transform us,
but the flaming sword above our heads
threatens to forgive us.

I rode the sea as a child, learned the names of every monster that approached the ship, watched sharks feast on what remained of a whale while her calf circled. Sailors told me tales of animals who lived beyond the sun's reach whose bodies manifested their own light.

Sanctus

We strip the midwife to prove her body is
like ours.
At night we tie her to
beams in the ceiling.
Bent under her spirit's arousal
she accuses us
even as we sever her tongue –

How can you say my prayers?

How dare you say the dead child
            in my room is your son?

        This is my devotion to the returning dead.
These are the ruins
            I mapped onto my body so I might always be
lost.

I lived past the day I was told I would die. The earth
didn't rupture. The sky didn't open. I am old enough now
to know we only love what will die for us. I don't want
to be forgiven for the stories I told; I want to forget the
bloodied yolk inside the broken egg. I am responsible to
what I have witnessed. I have eaten the eyes of the enemy,
and I am the enemy.

    Agnus Dei

We steal an hour from the future and burn
        all the books so history begins with us.

    We write:
            In the beginning light begat shadow,
        flowers begat fruit,
                but stars were fatherless.
        The wheat, radiant and unkind.

    We grow bored with paradise
        and take down the old commandments,
            but can't write new ones.

We sell each other stories of happiness
                but the pages are blank.

The starling starts to charge for its song,
its nest heavy with copper coins.

I know nothing of my father's myths, but my mother's parables are
sewn into my skirt. She gave me tarnished idols and her long shadow.
I come from a line of obedient women who want me to believe only
the strong lie under the stones they're given, but I am not buried
under the cairn. I am smearing blood on the lintels even though the
angel already passed over.

Lux Aeterna

Now, in the last world, we bury nightingales
                beneath the floor.
        Trackers with their ears to the ground listen
                for angels approaching.

Where is the saint,   mortally torn and wearing a hood of stars,
    bearing her own redemption –
      a heart of thorns   and a stone book?

      Rumors make women rush
            with tributes of roasted songbirds
                          to the fallen temples,
        but the epidemic continues.
        We remain empty.

Before they left
            priests tied laws to our wrists that said:
    Grief is a slow animal
            bearing an imperfect hope.

I try to name this feeling. This terrible lightness others call peace. I felt it once, watching bare trees, waiting for wary deer to approach the salt. Nothing sang. Bears gave birth in their sleep, and the cubs crawled out to admire their indigo shadows in the snow.

Libera Me

The doctors name our malady –
        Hysteria: suffering of the womb.

We want to be healed,
        relieved of our burden,
    so we remake our children   with clay, sing them
        lullabies and offer our breasts
    with the hesitation of new brides.

We let waves
        rock them past the shoals,
                set fire to our dresses
                        to transform ourselves
    into the ashes that pursue them across the sea.

I gave birth to a daughter, denied her three times, and when I found her at the ocean's edge, I wrapped her in a winding sheet and offered her to the man who walked toward me on the water.

JAMES BROOKES

FUNERAL CANTICLE FOR SIR JOHN TAVENER

At funerals you get this kind of thing:
'Music for God', new age, populist, bland,
then suddenly it's you, your eyes tear-stung,
the notes tremendous in another throat
you realise breathlessly is now your own;
divine dictation you can barely catch.
It's unsigned time like this that plays upon
the mind's deep reservoirs: organs of doubt
and faithfulness but above all else, sound:
the moment shifts from what it is about
to what you feel it is; the pitch comes down
something like a semitone beneath thought.
It stays with you, the frailty of it found
to have a measureless strength; at least, you ought
to know that when remembering a song
between your memory and your voice you're caught
short. But even the monadic drone
that's all that you can manage will support
grief and hope together in one tone.
You're speaking now a bit out of your depth;
it pulls you in the deep tow of its ison
as if you open up all notes at once
like an infant singing without tune.
Few moments of the thinking mind excuse this.
When you say you believe, you might put it to music.

JERICHO BROWN

PRAYER OF THE BACKHANDED

Not the palm, not the pear tree
Switch, not the broomstick,
Nor the closest extension
Cord, not his braided belt, but God,
Bless the back of my daddy's hand
Which, holding nothing tightly
Against me and not wrapped
In leather, eliminated the air
Between itself and my cheek.
Make full this dimpled cheek
Unworthy of its unfisted print
And forgive my forgetting
The love of a hand
Hungry for reflex, a hand that took
No thought of its target
Like hail from a blind sky,
Involuntary, fast, but brutal
In its bruising. Father, I bear the bridge
Of what might have been
A broken nose. I lift to you
What was a busted lip. Bless
The boy who believes
His best beatings lack
Intention, the mark of the beast.
Bring back to life the son
Who glories in the sin
Of immediacy, calling it love.
God, save the man whose arm
Like an angel's invisible wing
May fly backward in fury

Whether or not his son stands near.
Help me hold in place my blazing jaw
As I think to say excuse me.

N.M. BROWNE

IF GOD LURKS

If God lurks only in a poem's line
Called by the treble's arcing sound
He is no more than art's design,
A quality – like 'white' or 'round',
Cathedral based, a high aesthetic,
A bagatelle, a side show now.
No more the God of science, of ethics
The who, the why, the where and how.

But atoms of the mulitverse
Freeze with the bating of Her Breath.
Mock faith and call it cult or curse
It's early yet to laud its death.
God's source and sap and vital charge
Or nothing but a man dreamed large.

DIANA FITZGERALD BRYDEN

AN ATHEIST'S PRAYER

This year has seen the end of the world.
In dreams, processions of refugees unfurl
like snails, dragging the past on their backs.

Here in the city, glazed yellow,
pushed down in its bowl by the stinging heat,
I've been trying to translate my fear.
And to honour the dead,
whose dreams of the end are concrete.

First I went looking for prayers:
two men leave the plague-shocked city
at midnight, for a swim in the harbour.
The sky's milky, the water's warm.
The swimmers step into the sea's amen;
carry their burden, buoyant, between them.
In the grey night they drift, together,
through a passage of literature
so gentle, words become balm.

No gift could be better
than this compassionate diary,
which taught me to stay with what makes me afraid.
Camus felt the suffering of strangers; touching their sores,
he revealed his own soul's tender shores.
His words spread, like music,
– swim away, swim away, pain,
drift to the outer edges –
sombre and restrained.

This summer, a murdered girl's mother slips
into the jewel-blue of her pool.
She carries the burning – lets it float
from her; pain becomes more remote.
It moves out in ripples, into the city,
laps at the heels of reporters and readers,
who find it safer
to focus on one sorrow we've picked a name for
than on the reservoirs, open between us.

Tonight my city's a green bowl,
a cup of green, overflowing
whose light falls translucent, in watery veils.
A chorus is echoing, small and far-off,
and its quiet song reveals
a freshness that forgets nothing:
not death, not even murder.

JACCI BULMAN

ON A SITE SET BACK FROM THE ESTUARY

she's hanging washing
from her caravan window:
the old lady neighbour walks by.
They talk about summer coming,
the dogs last night, how Helen Fraser
is doing in California, then,
as she goes, the lady tells her
You have nothing to do in this life, love.
You are enough. And is gone.

She carries on placing T-shirts and
socks on the rail, looks up at the sky,
around the site, to see if someone
heard, or could explain. But there's
only the birds on the telegraph wire
above her, singing.

APRIL BULMER

RITES

I have sheared my hair
and my head is a full moon,
a light on my path.
I am a beacon for spirits
and frail ghosts,
though I love the Lord Jesus
and have prepared balms
and soft rags:
flannel cloth.

Oh to be a Sister,
to bear the cross,
the weight of His burden.
Instead, something this way comes:
a crow, his wing tipped in blood;
the moss at my feet
broken open like a woman;
twigs gathered in a ribbon;
the damp shadow of dog birth;
of men sinning.
I am a pagan
dreaming of the body of Christ:
taking the bread in my beak,
singing the rite.

STEPHEN BURT

FIRST ASTRONOMY GLOBE

Incapable of glowing
under my own light, I spin
instead. I do my best work when you are in bed,
either quiet & wide-eyed, or else asleep & unknowing,
& though I have an infinite supply
of darkness & silence, I let it all go by,
preferring not to scare you with the void.
I cut up my space into parts, & the parts fit in
to stories: *the boy who grew a giant fin,*
for example, & others you made up, *the anteater's tail,*
the trapezoid you named *the cellular phone* –
absurd or anachronistic, but no more so
than the camel, the hunter's belt and torso,
the dog star, the giant ladle, the lesser whale,
a cross to light the flags of southerly nations.
A wise
young gazer will memorise
not just the names for made-up constellations –
those dotted lines, those rules religions trace –
but the ranks of the stars themselves: keeping close to my face,
the attentive child past his bedtime sees
dim numbers that connect the faintest dots
to their glow-in-the-dark parameters, the plots
that cut my sphere
into right angles, minutes and degrees.
He finds in that firmament
no sign of human intent,
not even to ask what we are doing here.

CARMEN CALATAYUD

THE HOLY SPIRIT SPEAKS

I've stepped all over your prayers.
See blue corazón in the road.
This is your asking,
in the voice of Cuba spilling out of a cigar box.
Rich tobacco mixed with sand,
then scrubbing the streets of Sacred Heart.
Throw away your dialect,
and eat it for lunch.
Needing beads and chants, trinity touch and go.
Tricky spirits joking in their habitat.
They comb wet dark hair.
This corner of the street
sings glory, painful dust.
In ironed sleeves, there's dry anticipation.
Gypsy vision hangs inside these crazy bells.
Cherries spill across the stones,
a gift from Gabriel.
Pits tossed inside the sack,
sack holding, sack redeeming,
working without a cross.
Everybody's baptised
by the sun and that is all.

JASON CAMLOT

MY TEN COMMANDMENTS

I broke my 1st edition of the Ten Commandments
because I was extremely annoyed by something
(I can't remember...). I held it high
above my head, and then I smashed it
with all my might on the kitchen floor.
It shattered into more pieces than I could see.
When he heard what I did,
he was extremely angry with me, but
he did not smite me down where I stood.
Instead, he told me to promise I wouldn't do it again,
and then to build an ark to hold the covenant
I'd made with him. He told me
to place the new, 2nd edition of
the Ten Commandments, *carefully*, in
the ark. And not only that. He also ordered
me to collect every little shard of the broken
smashed and shattered 1st edition,
and to put them in the same
ark of the covenant as the new, 2nd edition.
When I asked him why, he said the
extremely broken and irreparable 1st edition
should be kept in this sacred and safe place,
to remind those who follow the commandments
how a broken, harmed, shattered, ill person
feels, as such a person still houses a spirit
equivalent to the spirit housed in his words,
but can no longer let the spirit speak as it should.
We are meant to know from an illegible soul
we shall never compare the 1st edition to the 2nd
for minute differences.

KIMBERLY CAMPANELLO

TO DISPLACE

To displace
the obelisk's
stacked stone
To invent new trumpets
tubas saxophones
To march
To attack first with rosemary
then predictions
To demand money
To accept tears
To run up the street
from our offices
in high heels
To grab our babies
To feed them
from our breasts
then and there
To light candles
in the grotto
To light so many
it will explode

MELANIE CHALLENGER

THE BEGINNING

First there was a mirror
That reflected itself and everything else there was
But couldn't look on its own image.
The mirror grew thin and improbable
Trying to see itself
It sprawled to every angle
A bodiless lens, a cellophane eye-piece
Become nothing but the hope of sight
Until the minute engine that made it
Surfaced, a love-knot in perfection, a tumour
Of mirrors, its oil was a thoughtless thought
Its mechanism was always to try and always
To fail to see itself.
For every catch-as-catch-can, it cast another mirror-skin
Each one smaller, more flawless
To sneak a view
Until time was invented as nothing more than this trial.
Each see-through flake took it to a whit,
Something slighter, tauter than its first rage
Until its failure burst out in uncountable shucks of frustration,
The hidden fault of faith in each one
Brought to light by sudden aggrandizement.

JOHN CHALLIS

THE RECTORS OF RAME

The piano and pump organ no longer work.
The back room stacked with worn candles,
the pulpit remembers the rectors,

pulling the bells and burning their palms
raising their arms in welcome,
villagers filling the aisles.

But now she enters, I make for the door,
and stop to watch her brush her hand
over every pew as though through corn,

and as she sits and stares
and bows her head in prayer,
she is welcomed by what I cannot see.

PATRICK CHAPMAN

PROTECTION

You tell me of a guardian that follows us by day
and stalks us in the night. It writes what it observes

into a reckoning ledger. It passes that intelligence
on to its master, the one who has always known

what the angel will report; who made spacetime
to run in all directions in a manifold universe;

who gave us the sun and the echoing moon;
who left us the earth and in its crust embedded

dinosaur fossils to test our belief,
while he also made Darwin.

He constructed this world according to our needs
yet allows us to be stricken with the birth defect

of original sin, that guilt which may be expiated
only through our murder of his son,

as when a dealer in narcotics offers *gratis*
the first taste of heaven.

The merciful creator whose wrath we must fear,
demands all our love lest he burn us forever.

He gave us free will but sanctions damnation
for heeding the devil he made as his agent.

Omnipotent, omniscient, encompassing
eternal being as well as nonexistence

– for if everything is possible, nothing is required –
he is complicit in all that we are, all that we do;

and if true to his own law, would cast himself out.
Tell me again by what name I should call that old beast.

SAMPURNA CHATTARJI

COMPANION PIECE

Doubt

Perhaps one day my absolute ignorance will lead me towards you
Weakest at the moment when I write I snarl when anyone enters the room
Show my claws like a neutered she-cat a bandage tight around my belly
A collar round my neck so I cannot lick my wounds

What I haven't learnt is how to look into a human's eyes unafraid
That all my pain will be discovered in this instant of animal connection
Whiskered breath on my cheeks unblinking recognition
Stay away stay away there is a much crueller beast afoot

Faith

This is a dead wood its colour ash
We walk through it holding conversation like hands
There the dust of a passing car brings travelers
Who disembark, the woman takes our photo, amazes her men
With her ability to take pictures and charm us with her smile
The girls hide their cigarettes.

We can be reserved and hilarious together.
We can sing, or laugh, or weep, standing in the dead wood
Or sitting in the room where tears arrive unannounced, embarrassing
Only the one who sheds them
Arms around her like a forest of sheltering shadows
The murmur of leaves against her wet cheeks.

The next morning she wakes into herself, an 'I' again, and says
To the field where the fog hangs and three cows gently low:

Here I am, ready to be made over in some material other than flesh.
Ready to see not the shifting silence but the speaking glance.
Ready to laugh with again, not at.
Here I am, a line of clothes hung out to dry in yesterday's dead wood,
Small, intimate, necessary,
And the wood suddenly alive, and beautiful.

AYESHA CHATTERJEE

KETAKI

I wanted to tell you about the white flower
that drifted down a pillar of light

and rendered a god faceless,

but what do I really know
except that temples are dotted with beggars and cow dung
and that I would scream in terror

if I were to see a man with an elephant's head?
It takes a woman to wear the scent of divinity
in her hair and at the base of her throat.

It takes a god to call that cursed.

MAXINE CHERNOFF

OFFERINGS

A cluster of belfries encants the human idea. – Rimbaud

The heart-shaped meteorite is not message or omen, talisman or cure.
Locket of the world's intention, correlation of tangent and bone:
The church in Bruges where the blood of Christ thickened in a vial is
      chained to a priest.
Death on vacation, a humid Sunday when he says something trifling,
then looks at her for the final time.
Who notices that a train leaves unless it is bound for grief?
The man who said he'd been blinded but now could see he had kept
      the knowledge of failing to himself.
His blue eyes told of the miracle, which meant he would keep reading
      Yeats to students
who Twitter and text during his lectures, who read box scores and
      Google their names.
Heart from the sky, blood in the vial, fragments of what's said,
left over beauty on a train to Bruges become story by connecting the dots:
Words flee, wanting a home in another context. Let's build
a reliquary where, under indigo velvet and gilded lining, they
      can escape prying eyes.

CAROLINE CLARK

BEAUTIFUL LOSS

Over in un–
cut autumn
light all before
and possible
pouring in

there in golden
so fleeting
settled peace
comes to a place
passed
unnatural I may
be this is magnified
life   I
follow for
but seconds

its scent on
me all life-
long   looking
and losing
looking and losing.

PATRICIA CLARK

CREED

I believe in one body, ligaments almighty, skin
wrapping the thankful bones, and the resurrection
of the stomach, waking to hunger each day
with dreams of basil and butter, fennel, old gouda
cheese, and wine poured like sunlight into glass.
I believe in the fretting of shadow and sun
on backyard grass, in the shedding of the oak,
in the temptation of an umbrella on the deck,
a table, a chair, and an opened book.
The ascension into light, especially after lying down
with another, causes us to sit at the right
hand of whatever spirit guides us, called love
by some believers. And I believe in perennials,
bark, moss instead of grass, the pollen stuck
on a stamen, the hyssop turning blue as the night.

GEORGE ELLIOTT CLARKE

SPIRITUALS 1: 1-7

God never says no mumblin word:
Cryin for Christ, crossed, His tears thundered.

Our Good God be a Man of War –
He sits in Heaven and judges prayer.

I hate the Cross, that accursèd tree
Made my Lamb's blood drip like honey.

But look at Jesus now, scribin Poesy –
Bright sparkles sear the furthest sky.

Wily as Homer, that reverend Bard
Gleans soulful sweets from His lyric orchard.

Ol Adam and Eve, like us, were black:
They fell into Hell, but Christ hauled em back.

Take out your pencil; pick up the Book –
These measures save us once-damned folk.

[New York City (New York) 23 janvier mmxi]

GERALDINE CLARKSON

ON A HILL

On a hill, I always thought, I'd have an encounter, woman
to God; or in the candled calm of some huge-statued
basilica, its sparkling dark. Perhaps at a tree-
starved shrine, with pilgrims stretched in crocodile;
or in bed – through the night – like in Psalm 63.
Maybe via an angel, masquerading
as a stranger. Or in the bath,
public or private – it's not unheard of.

But – *en la poesía* – how could it happen? –
pen and paper prodding to prayer – to prepare.

Just as father Abraham, with the promise of offspring
plenty as stars – offered sacrifice:
animals caught, blood-let, slaughtered, halved, set out in a line.
Before the flames came.

AIDAN COLEMAN

ON THE TRANSPORTATION OF THE NORTH WINDOW *

Dismantle the beards and the odd feet,
the green of date palms and paned faces,
the urgent sky's banner and
dinner plate haloes;
fracture with care the
bended knees, the fingers pointing
to already over.
Dis-piece the wing-stumps
of angels' shoulders, blunt Christ's aphorisms:
Word from word;
flat-pack and taxi through electric dusk,
to rise again in the East.

* Some time early in the twentieth century the altar window of St. Peters' Cathedral
in North Adelaide was taken down and reassembled in St. Bart's Anglican Church in
Adelaide's Eastern Suburbs.

NANCY COOK

WRITTEN IN NATURE

i

God spoke to me: All creation speaks my name.
I am creator, I must create.
I must create
as God created, created in nature. Nature as written by God,
nature as will be written through me, through me, Antoni Gaudí.
Trees will rise, branches spread, fruit fatten aburst with colors not
imagined but in the mind of God. A place of worship rising,
rising up on creatures' backs:
tortoise shells stronger than boulders, stronger than mountains,
stronger than sin. A falling leaf
staircase: leaves falling, captured in their fall, in time inconsequential.
Light and shadow and black, windowed by design, math and myth
and line, birth and betrayal and death. The ways of nature, nature
written by God. God is speaking, speaking to me, revealing
what God could create, what God will create, through me.

ii

God spoke to me: Here is where I live; here you must live. You must
remain faithful, you must remain here. You must speak, as I speak to
you, John Muir. Here you will save me in my glory. Here in falling
water is the power of falling; here on this rock face, the face of God,
the power
of endings, of facing the end; here in the redwoods, the red blood of
ancients, reminder of time,
the awful humility of human time. There at branches' end, the
ends of earth, skies of black, the heavens' black, pierced by millions
of angels' eyes. Men will seek to be great here, men will seek my
greatness, seek to be greater, to vanquish the walls, rock face, face of
God, to seize and quell the waters; men will seek to trounce the trees,
to humble the redwoods, expose

the skies to gawkers. But God will not allow, God must not
permit, lights made by humans
to cancel the lights of angels.

iii
I saw the crowds, strings of bodies waiting to get in. I saw the
buses. I saw the guidebooks, cameras, carabiners, backpacks, ticket
stubs, handheld guides with earphones, water bottles,
trail mix, sketch pads, souvenirs. I saw parades of bankers, money
handlers, entrepreneurs, and conmen. Everyone was speaking.
I fled.

iv
I followed nothing but my soles. I walked. I walked on train
tracks, county roads, ship decks, blue-blazed trails; I threaded
tunnels, staggered over rope and concrete bridges. I roamed
with pilgrims, bore with witnesses, kept company with crusaders,
eco-tourists, tramps. I followed every pathway, paths of pioneers,
explorers' paths, the ways of refugees and nomads, lost souls, on
sand, on grass, on ice. I lost the way. I lost my faith. I lost myself.
Insensible, I discovered nowhere underneath a naked sun, beside a
stand of trees, trees as tall as ambitions, with leaves
as broad as welcome mats. I slept on padded pine, pillow of
flowers, colors pillowing, all colors
of the spring, randomly arranged. For my ears, comfort: crickets,
songbirds, frogs, coyotes in the distance, rush of leaves, trickling,
tumbling cascades and creeks. I slept surrounded, stars all around,
stars abounding, angels' eyes. Falling, a leaf adrift. A leaf adrift,
falling. And God said welcome, welcome here; you are welcome.

ALFRED CORN

ANTHONY IN THE DESERT

To be filled with that hallowed emptiness
The hermit sojourns in a desert cave.
Fasting and prayer will make seclusion safe,
His daily bread, each word the Spirit says.

Chimera stirs and rears her dripping head;
A slack-skinned reptile puffs and makes a face;
Vile, harrowing nightmares glimmer through long days;
The sun beats a brass gong and will not set.

Faint shadow on cave walls, you foretell grief
Or joy, not known till whose the profile is:
Love itself may corrupt and then deceive
Its object, hiding venom in a kiss.
Anthony kneels, embraces his fierce lot,
And hears: *Be still, and know that I am God*.

RACHEL COVENTRY

BEAT

Systole

I am still living at all the old addresses
unable to see skin deep improvements,
wandering pre-gentrified Stoke Newington
lost in a maze of grey council estates
still transfixed by reverberations
of tower blocks that have not yet
shivered to the ground
but still sweep acid house,
a lonely beam over
Hackney's waste ground.

Diastole

Burning like the earth
at the Burmese border
the fans all noise no effect
Thai women, still as Buddhas,
me, huffing and bloated
wrestling with Christ on the floor,
really grasping at straws,
weaving pale meanings from gecko calls.
Maybe I'll take succor in a different boy?
Some ragged memory blazes momentarily
leaves me destitute. Giving in, finally, I breathe.

CLAIRE CROWTHER

EPITHALAMIUM

Look, love: a treasury for us
to curate together.
But more than the valuables of travels
is their cabinet.
It weds us in its walls out of the world.
A brimful stoup.
A paten that carries our linen. Does it matter
what great containers
are made of? Wood, pewter or silver
whose waterfalls
of shine stream down the sides of chalices?
Love, our marriage
will absorb the light of all things
inside gems.

TONY CURTIS

AT GUMFRESTON CHURCH

That evening, after a hard, hot drive,
The dark lane's coolness of trees
Was like water walked into,
Calm and quiet – no traffic,
Deep shadows,
All the gulls out at sea.

Augustus and Gwen's father
Walked the two miles from Tenby
Every Sunday to play the organ here.
I search for his headstone and find no-one
But Ken Handicott the grocer
I worked for one school summer holiday
Forty years ago.

They leave the church door unlocked:
There is no congregation but the curious passing folk.
And inside is the simple splendour of stone font,
Low wooden roof, draped altar, Norman-built
On earlier significance – St. Teilo, St. Bridget.
The place shivers in the dusk
And moves into another night.
Here were the early missions, saints and sinners
Crossing the Irish Sea, moving east
With their crosses and swords.
Here was a quay, a village the river Ritec
Joined to the sea that led to the world.

And here, behind the church, before the woods
Where the Magdalens brought their lepers,
Still flow the three springs of purity

And healing, coming to us from a depth.
Water that plays the oldest music.
Without thinking
I take a handful
And with wet, cool fingers
Cross myself.

CYRIL DABYDEEN

BELIEVERS

Catechism of the right and left,
Censers moving in smoke-filled air
Because of what's always true

Faith we carry to a place called
Heaven; and pain, oh pain,
As I come to the Cross with

Bread of the body, blood of
A river: Babylon with the one
Named John I now tell about

Baptism tied to the senses, or
Being in a real heaven I've come
To believe in all these years

PÁDRAIG J. DALY

INCARNATION

1.
We would have done it otherwise:

We would have kept the fluttering messengers,
The journey in haste,
The wondrous birth.

Pity is important;
So we would have allowed him pain
And pity.

We would have kept the feasting,
The sinner companions,
The softness of God.

But what need was there
For the garden agony, the nails through the palms,
The roars from the cross?

2.
Feeling as men and women feel,
Quaking before pain
As men and women quake,

He entrusts Himself to the High Father
As men and women entrust themselves
To human constancy;

And, trusting that luminous love,
He edges on
To the blind halt of death.

3.
That all of this – sun, water's rush,
Men and women moving, haloed, through the streets –
Came from nothing, nowhere, nobody,
I cannot credit; so believe.

It is afterwards I balk:
Mind-melting Otherness?
Or Otherness-Made-Flesh,
Softly among us?

4.
And, being man,

Did he think, as men and women thought,
That Jonah dwelt three days within the whale,
Immune to belly juices?

That devils lived flamboyantly inside the sick
And, when his heart was moved to heal,
Left them, yelping?

That the world soon,
With hail and lightning bolt,
Must end?

How did he forsee
The horror of his dying,
The direful future of Jerusalem?

And how much grasp unknowable God,
Bending in his flesh
To pitch among us?

5.
With human arms
Grappling each of myriad us to human heart,
There stilling us,

The love that flows from Father-God,
And all God's joy,
Holds each of us, through Him,

In an Embrace,
Where every dotish one of us
Is marvellous and singular,

Where there is no longer need
For talk or explanation, gestures of regret;
Just simple surrender to our God's delight.

PETER DANIELS

GOD'S POWER

Do I have God in mind? Am I talking to him?
Is he listening? Is that an easy pronoun
or a long way round?

Here's where I am. Careful about reality
while I hold the door to the outside world
from there to the stars.

God could perhaps part the waves because
the waves are part of him, like the ones
Jesus defied with his feet.

There's a story of sacrifice. There's a story
of everything coming right, if we can make it
come to anything at all.

People have carved oak and marble to show
how the flesh was pierced, the body held up
and left there to die.

This never drew me to God. God had other ways
he could reach me by leaving me alone to play
with the rest of the world.

That is, all of the world, and I'm here in it now
with my body made of it, and my soul beating
with my blood and breath.

God might grieve when I die – how I would
like to think so – but God will continue to be
all that exists.

I part the sea a little. I stop to warn myself
I could be drowning. There is a life to keep
moving along with.

Like a wave met by a passing boat, and like
the wave the boat makes as it passes through,
the water continues.

COLIN DARDIS

POSITIONS TO GOD

I had read Luke, and considered
how far I was from God,
not at His left hand, or right.

Perhaps placed at His hip,
slobbering like an upset child
pleading to mother for comfort.

To be at His brow, although
I have no perfume, sent away
in tender resignation.

To be at His feet, if tears
could sluice out from me,
honouring my station.

Here is truth: there is not a loaf
baked in this world that could tame
my famine; I feed on prayer instead.

GRAHAME DAVIES

DISILLUSION
Simone Weil

Never to trust again,
not a priest, not a politician,
not a mentor, not an author,
not a lover, not a friend.
And not myself,
certainly not myself.
Never to give again,
not my money, unquestioning,
not my hope, undoubting,
not my time, unstinting.
And not my love,
no, certainly not my love.
Because they all fail;
dream more than they can do,
promise more than they can be,
believe that they are better than they are.
We all do.
And what is best of us
dissolves like incense in a chancel.
And now, knowing this,
expecting nothing,
wanting nothing,
fearing nothing,
to trust, to give, to love.

HILARY DAVIES

GOD'S OVEN

God's oven, that summer.
The land was turned to straw
And the trees tinder.
The white road led through the white wheat.
Men fell in love with silence in the consuming heat.

When does the door open?
How does the ear prepare
For what it does not even know
It cannot hear?

Some little slip, some little tear
Ajar things as they are,
Or seem to be.
Like tiny acorns breaking up the ground,
Their filaments as delicate as spiders' webs,
Root with power to raise a colossus.
So I crossed into church after church that summer,
Thinking of erudition, but beside me trod Love.
O my unrecognised familiar, subtle of subtles,
Showing with open palm the forms
To piece together to learn the inlay of faith.

Ligugé's the place where understanding
First ran over the stones like water evermore,
Where the renounced of the world in their radiating chapels
Hoisted eleison, and my spirit trembled at the door.

FLORA DE FALBE

ST. PAUL'S
after David Bomberg

Wars licked up the colour,
charred the angels on their pedestals.
Now it grows straight out of the pavement,
a dark-windowed moan of a thing:
haunted by trees, hassled
by a sky of TV static.
Morning scrubs its edges,
and a spire extends like a talon
to gouge out the sun.
Dawn is bald as eyeball-whites.
Birds dissolve in the light.
Now a car trickles by, now a cat.
We are testing our feet in case they fall apart,
carbonised; we want the rain
to make the streets clean,
but it stagnates in puddles.
Dear Lord, we are very tired.
Please send a lightning bolt,
or some sign that you're all right.

JAN DEAN

THE KINGDOM OF GOD

The kingdom of God is like
a man who buys a bargain basement shrub
and plants it in his garden.
And when it grows
it is not a small and tidy thing
it is horse chestnut
alive with lime green leaves
and tall pink candle flowers
its roots will wreck the footings
of his house.
And when he sees this great tree
shoot into the air
a solid fountain
pouring shushing foliage
and sparking blossom flames
the man's eyes widen
and he roars with laughter.
Such is the kingdom of God.

JOHN F. DEANE

NAME AND NATURE

Your name, Jesus, is childhood in the body, at times
A single malt upon the tongue, Vivaldi to the ears;

your name, Christ, forgiveness to the heart, acceptance
to the flesh, a troubled joy across the soul

at ever my very best I will plead to you, closest to me
for kindness. Perhaps the silence I take for God's

non-presence is the noise in which I have immersed
my life; nor have I framed a quiet to correspond

to His, where I might find my every call
answered. I seek kind. You are the reality I cling to,

the flesh, the history, the spurting out of blood. I believe
the non-attendance of my God lies in my absence from Him

and He is present, like the embrace of air
or the inward forces of the seasons. Your name, Jesus,

is the river on which I float, your name, Christ, the ocean
where everything is in place, is shivering, beautiful, and apart.

NICHOLA DEANE

YESTERDAY'S CHILD

Sorrow and rage, rage and sorrow
are beads on a thread of ragged prayer

and yesterday's child can't cut the string
and her life is strung on thin thin air

she ever doggedly sowing tomorrow
with sorrow and rage and rage and sorrow

NATASHA DENNERSTEIN

SUBMISSIVE

Take my lips, my guts, my heart
and do with me what you will:
I have been your creature from the start.

I've given up fighting; it was tearing me apart.
I'm exhausted; I've been through the mill,
so take my lips, my guts, my heart.

In this melodrama I took the wrong part
and this fighting and fighting has made me ill.
I have been your creature from the start.

I put the horse before the cart;
I did stupid things just for the thrill.
Now take my lips, my guts, my heart.

To tell the truth, I was a stupid tart
and if it wasn't for you I'd be carrying on still.
I have been your creature from the start.

Then you told me you had something to impart:
I listened and am listening still.
So take my lips, my guts, my heart:
I have been your creature from the start.

DHARMAVADANA

ACROSS THE LAKE

a holy congregation of pines
awaits an answer

but the water's sparkling children
distract me.

Behind me the lane
seeps on through the valley.

A beech tree's shadow
passes like a radius.

U.S. DHUGA

FOOLS LIKE ME

Am I not ridiculous,
listening to the susurrus
of wind among my Norway Maple's leaves
and fancying it grieves
the end of us.
For only fools like me believe
that when the loved one leaves
her ghost will always haunt the purlieus
of his silent house
like timid thieves.

JOSEPHINE DICKINSON

HOW CAN I EXPLAIN TO YOU THAT HE WAS REAL?

In a lump which banged as it humped,
the last of the lamb came out of the freezer,
deliquesced in the summer heat
in a bowl overnight. Next morning
it slid from its bag, unwrapped
from its thick aroma. With thumbs I prised
the red pool, wet and sweet, ripped
white sinews off a strip of breast meat,
ran the kidneys out of their marble sheath,
found a scrap of liver, drizzled the earth
and shit off the feet with a jet of icy water.

He said:
'Now for the opening up of the heart,
the hollow chamber. You have to open the heart.
Tear the calms from the crucible stains
in the middle, trim off the fat.
Slice it through and open it out
through the wall, the medallions,
blazons of light, the doors which open
on one side only. Reveal the left
and right apartments, the best of rooms,
the choice, the best of the house,
wherein to feed, to lodge, to love.'

EDWARD DOEGAR

SOMETHING UNDERSTOOD

Be seated. So much silliness. Go in fear
      of imperatives. Love,
as much as anything else, as little.
      Stop trying to touch
the stained light, it's not for you. Feel
      the wood instead; use
has polished the grain, this is not good,
      this is not evil. Wood
is also stained. And so on. Deliver us
      from this, from that.
From our petty convictions. Is it true
      that belief makes
something true? If only here? If
      only. Listen: the hinge
of restlessness caught in a pew, a child
      itching to join in. Give
us this day our daily bread. Forgive
      us our trespasses.
How many mouths has this mattered to?
      How many has it fed?
Enough. Find the light, the door. Be sated.

SHARON DOLIN

LET ME THRUM (6 A.M.)

a new lay upon this lute for you
Let me hum the new day
of loose strife and lily

Let prayer plant and mallow
Let heads and hearts   let heels
and thumbs   feathers and fins
and all things fleet and slug

antennae'd and furred
all sing all shirr all rub and buzz
and fling their call to you
in song-light as the mist still clings

as the settled dew thins
as all attendant things

in your rising yolk-red grin
unfold and re-begin.

TIMOTHY DONNELLY

MONASTIC

The ruined cathedral wept into my flesh
because I held nothing within me with warmth
enough to deflect it. I flattened a hand
against its relief to imagine the hand
that had carried it out –
the cuff, the garment, the quick
scent of limestone struck into shape
and the whimper of cooling.
I carried myself with all I imagined
down to a lake, letting

are you   are you
loose over water, out in the air –
how incomprehensible
being has been to me
from the beginning – and back
to the rock, laying all of it

down – slant wood overhead
that would moulder away,
the cowl, the calling, I can hear
the voice carried back to me,
lessoned, my own
blown voice, blowing   there   there

MAURA DOOLEY

GROTTO

Shell spangled
with the crusty shadow of death,

undergrowth
    spliced and wired
to make a bower,
reined in,
    espaliered wilderness,
crown of thorns,
      empty chamber,

through which the wind sighs
like a long withdrawing sea.

TIM DOOLEY

PRAYER
After Boethius

Star-maker, world conductor,
turbine of the rapid turning
sky, moon-pacifier that stills
the satellite to rest in sun –
letting it pale in the off weeks,
letting the beauty of the lesser
lights shine within its darkened horns –
force that in the evening's first
moments sends Venus chasing
the frigid stars across the
dark blue, violet and indigo
backdrop, until she rises
shamefaced, pale as Lucifer
in the morning-fresh sky;

thermostat of the globe,
force that, when the winter
finally lets leaves fall, limits
our view of their crisp curled
burial to the shortest hours and
in summer's violent heat,
when the body calls out for love,
quickens the passage of dark;
what the North Wind strips
from elm and oak and beech
the Gulf Stream soothes into bud;
what was sown in the days of
the Joy Star, the dog days will
see toasting in full crop;

if everything in nature points
to underpinning laws that
run inside the veins and reach
the distant stars, why have
all made and living things
been turned to whims of chance,
so that winds pull trees
from their roots, the sea rises
against us, the poles weep?
Why has human desire
played with the balance
of things so that no-one
can judge the weight of
a coin in justice's hands?

CAL DOYLE

WHERE I'M FROM

I am from the Pleiades
and you cannot see me
behind the shifting formations
of night clouds

I am from the closing credits
of your favourite film
I know your neck
and it is weak

I am from her eyes
when she told you
that she would love to
but perhaps in another life

I am from the brick walls
that receive licks of paint
and bloodied heads clenched by fists
in tangles of hair

I am from the light
split and spat by glass and crystal
onto your face, feel me
stay right there

IAN DUHIG

MARGERY KEMPE'S

Beneath her white wool pilch, the trial hair shirt
she cut from malt-nets rotted with her tears.
Her husband later burned their kiln in rage
when he grasped what she meant by cleanliness.

While suffragans grilled her for Lollardry,
gnawed her visions like rats gnawing stockfish,
she prayed to Margaret of Antioch
who exploded the dragon which ate her.

The pilgrim's shell instructed her in tongues
miraculously strange to every land.
In Jerusalem she learned how to scream
and was roasted for Flagellantism.

She returned with the bull for the church font,
with dreams of a bear which gorged on blossom
to fart storms of petals at priestly spies.
Her neighbours called this the cheese parable.

Tap the ribs of this her burned-out poem
as she tapped the dovecote of Christ's body,
you'll cry with soot-falls from her brewing-kiln,
with falling dust, scales and white, white feathers.

FRANK DULLAGHAN

EVEN IN THE MIDST OF GRIEF

Even in the midst of grief the hands break
bread, the mouth eats. Even in grief,
the body has its small circle of comfort –
a cool bed, sun blessing the face.
The future continues to sail in
with its hold and its decks full.
It may transport greater levels of pain
or it may bring joy. Even in the midst of grief
the body walks the shore gathering stones;
gathering the wide sea into the heart.

Even when the heart thinks life is over,
one could come who will change all
that has gone before. Just as each new wave
washes the previous one away.

SUSAN MILLAR DUMARS

UNDISCOVERED

We lie together quietly
in our big boat of a bed.
His toenail, kneecap, hipbone,
the warm, wet tang of him.
The familiar soft spell
of his voice. *Now that I've seen death,*
I don't know how anyone
can think there's a God.

I see what he is seeing:
the final clench of jaw, the last
mute struggle, the leak of colour
starting at the hairline.
The way the lips fall open,
dumb. The nurse tucks a rolled cloth
beneath the chin to close the mouth.
We're machines, we break down.
Nothing more. Nothing else.

I remember her body
just after – shrunk,
the skin a new skin,
cold and slack as a white sail
on a windless day.
Something had gone. Though we can't
see the breeze, we know when
it stops blowing. Something had gone.
I only want to know what it was.

JOE DUNTHORNE

THE MONKS

One night the bells start to peal
inside them. Perhaps they are hearing
God think and since He is ever thoughtful
they lie awake, mirroring the clapper
with their tongues until a cloudless dawn
slides a lancet through the air above each bed.

Hours later they share a ward: twelve appendices
in St. Bart's incinerator. Some of their number
fear morphine will stretch a membrane
between them and their suffering.
One gives in and discovers God's beneficence,
on his feet in hours, retraining as a paralegal.

Those who pass the test return to the minster,
eyes throbbing behind polarized shades,
guided by a non-conceptual pain,
tracing the cloister walls.
A God that wants
for no disciples is no kind of God at all.

ANNA DWYER

REASON

Everything happens for a reason
she said
and reasonably I listened
and thought yes
you take an action there is a consequence
you take no action there is a consequence
rationally
I nursed my broken brain
and know that it broke
like so many brains before it
because it knows that the Universe
doesn't care
sends nothing
weaves no fate
does not fail to intercede
because it never intended to participate
I'll send you good karma
she said
and I smiled
unable to muster up
the mandatory thanks
thinking only that
the rational number
is
zero.

MICHAEL EGAN

ASH WEDNESDAY
for Noah

Child, let them mark your forehead with a cross
of black ashes if that's what needs to be done.
Know that the echo of your heart's beating
is the same: a temporary mark, a Sacramental murmur.
If faith is what's needed then have the faith to turn
from sin or temptation or nothing and if you find
Christ there then let him be with you, indelible and often,
or if not then let life be your Christ; a miracle
of being here, of coming through and seeing.
As the day wears on let your forehead remain stained.
I would always rub my own ashes away, wet a finger
and call their removal an accident, a careless smudging.
Remember you were dust once but don't be sullied
by that revelation and when you find the world
covered with layers of dust then question that
but treat what you discover beneath those layers
as curiosities; abstain from holding on to what you find,
don't greedily consume what you alone might know.
And when you come home with God still clinging
to your tongue, drink water to quench your thirst,
remember when the finger pressed to your forehead
there were remnants in the ash of what was burnt,
an echoing, faint smell; how ash was something once.

SAM EISENSTEIN

WHAT DREAMS

What dreams may come/when we have shuffled off this mortal coil – Shakespeare, *Hamlet*

A dream of eternal togetherness
with those lost, both so suddenly,
within a few days of each other

The shock divides consciousness
like two separated particles
indivisible despite separation

Of the living and the departed
but to where, to when, and why?
those I've lost belong together

My virgin love, my precious dog,
gravely introduced, now allies,
urging me to regard them,

Skipping over familiar ground
not seen for half a century,
but neither of them cares,

Because each of them carries
some invisible part of me,
and I may hope it's their heart

That pumps my name staccato
while engaged in happy exertion,
their gladness at finding one another

In the mystery of after-life,
because as we know there isn't
any except for memory.

ALISON ENGLEFIELD

A BUTTERFLY GOES TO CHURCH

With a soft beat for freedom,
a red admiral rises slowly,
wings pattering against the panes.
She hovers above the altar,
and settles on the crumbling plaster
that clutches at the sodden wall.
Here, an absent spider
once wound an optimistic web,
but left for sunnier climes.
One long strand of dusty silk
curls around her leg,
tethers her, a velvet kite.
Intense fluttering flakes the paint.
Like snow it falls in slow-motion,
in and out of daggers of light.
One determined twist
and she is free to fly
within this cold prison.
She presses to the glass;
belly warming in a flash of sun,
bright wings back-lit black.
Below, tiny particles of stucco
waft and sink, circling the cross
with a halo of white.

MICHAEL FARRY

A PRESENT FROM AMERICA

She specified a crucifix not a cross;
the body, she explained, that's the difference.
We had great difficulty, bare wood everywhere
in the Californian religious goods emporium
and marble, plastic, even rubber.
I almost asked the grinning servant girl
if she had a hidden stash for deviant customers
but her cheerfulness spooked me
so I bought two CDs of Christian rap, fled.

We forgot about it then until the last day.
In desperation we plodded the dark alleys,
searched the down-town dives
of hardly-legal hucksters,
sifted through forsaken treasures
and there it was, tarnished, no chain,
the upright bent, but a crucifix.
I tried to hide my glee, failed, paid thirty dollars.

Her delight was muted but sincere.
I saw her once in a public house
show it off – her American present
which crossed the Atlantic
the opposite way to her two brothers.

When she died last year
I suggested
it be buried with her
but they refused.

It's lighter than it looks,
gentle on my neck,
the body no extra burden.

JANETTE FERNANDO

INCARNATION

God of my universe
did you google earth
and come zooming in
to a particular place
at a particular time
to a particular girl,
chosen with care?

God of my nakedness
who formed me before birth,
how could you allow
your own son
to be stripped so bare
that he, who was not created
but Co-Creator,
should be born of one of us,
become one with us,
become one of us?

God of my self
who bared his own son,
do you invite me
to bear him now,
to carry the seed of Hope
who will take over my self
and bear me?

ANNIE FINCH

EVE

When mother Eve took the first apple down
from the tree that grew where nature's heart had been
and came tumbling, circling, rosy, into sin,
which goddesses were lost, and which were found?
What spirals moved in pity and unwound
across our mother's body with the spin
of planets lost for us and all her kin?
What serpents curved their mouths into a frown,
but left their bodies twined in us like threads
that lead us back to her? Her presence warms,
and if I follow closely through the maze,
it is to where her remembered reaching spreads
in branching gifts, it is to her reaching arms
that I reach, as if for something near to praise.

NORMAN FISCHER

NOBODY

Almost not going to concerts alone, I'm with nobody,
Not bothering to discuss the music either
You can't really discuss the music anyway
Even with somebody
All-pervasively and whole-heartedly

The dancer on the ceiling takes no prisoners
Thus escaping detection by the ghost brigades
That have been hanging around the auditorium
Formerly off limits except to luminous shepherds
And so compose the notices we love to scorn

Nobody follows through anymore
Nobody makes plans
Nobody cares

Forces don't balance, they oppose
Producing winners and losers at every turn
That depend on each another for their supposedly clear names
Thus generating reactivity to segue into forced choice
That gets kicked all the way down to the next corner
Where the Korean grocer awaits the immaculate robbery

To harness all that as you think you should
Would be to oppose the world
To try to think your way through an extrapolating embankment
So as to escape
Back to the future,
Where it's perpetually cooler than it is here

Might as well be spring – or Poland –
Might as well relax and stop swimming
The current will pull you where you need to be

The party of the first part is no party at all
And never was a part of any party

Nobody knows the trouble I've seen

ADAM D. FISHER

TOUCHING

When the Torah is carried
the young woman without a ring,
the man with a cane,
the gentleman wearing a silk suit, kiss
their tallit they've touched
to the Torah – like touching God, like touching
a talisman, like shaking hands
with a doctor hoping healing will rub off, like
touching the sleeve, the shoulder, the face
of someone they love.

CHARLENE FIX

VISITATION

I dreamed my father came back
looking macerated, mostly a voice,
but unmistakably his timbre.
I asked him, 'What's it like?'
He said, 'You can forget about
the Big Man, but there are lots
of Lesser Authorities'. This came
not, I am certain, from my head,
that believes in a Central Light
whose chief virtue is Unmyopic
Sanity, but was my father's
singular message to me,

or something, perhaps, from Cocteau.

SARAH FLETCHER

THE GIFT SHOP FIGURINES OUTSIDE ST. MARY'S CHURCH

The clay's too cheap to hold a sculpted face
and so the statue-Mary never weeps.
And while the Christ is splayed about her feet,
her face remains slate-blank and holds no shape.
Her Joseph's not lamenting. No one pays
for these featureless figurines, a cheap
Pietà moment. A faceless Holy scene.
This Mary always stares upon the vase;
but we know, in truth, that statues never think
or stare or watch their buyers walk away.
No matter the emotion on the ink,
they'll know not that their limbs will break when bought,
because their Maker sought a cheaper clay.

PIOTR FLORCZYK

PSALM

When you visit
again, Lord, please
take everything

that is not here
to stay, to be
long after me.

See, all my junk
has been sorted,
scooped and neatly

stacked in three piles
against the wall.
This stained futon,

this wobbly chair
and the coffee
table, can be

carried at once
upon your back.
All the tools of

my crime are here,
packed in the wood
box sealed and nailed

shut for the road.
Read the labels —
not in Coptic,

Aramaic,
but in plain speech
of zeroes, ones –

it will help You
decipher my
notes, thoughts, even

some bars of rage
written at night
in the margins

of books, white sheets
that my lovers
never found soft.

You see, I read
somewhere that we
are nothing but

fertilizer
for History, for
what's yet to come.

How funny then
that I now sit
leaning, blocking

my exit door.
Will you knock three
times, ring the bell?

Until you come,
pardon my dust,
my paper hat,

the fact that I,
dear Lord, kill time
tasting the hard

candy of your
body trembling
inside my mouth.

JAMES FLYNN

PROMISED LAND

Nothing covenanted or scriptural
Was vouchsafed me or even hinted at
But now that I have travelled there, I know
That had I not –

Had I not been drawn away from my map
To that dark passage way, that private gate,
And made welcome, a man both recognised
And awaited,

In that unimagined courtyard garden,
Soothed and revivified by the fountain
At the heart of the holy city, shown
The Temple Mount,

The Sea of Salt, the wilderness – had those
Sacramental encounters not occurred –
I'd have lived in unvoiced lack no less cruel
Than broken words.

JOHN FORBIS

SUSCIPE ME

There is a moment
in white, when
the mist clings,
and birdsongs cease,
when two hands grip a
breviary with ribbons set,
a monk's nervous fingers
end their motion,
when eyes freeze
on a floor pattern
and yet, no longer see it
and breathing stops.
That moment,
right before rising to stand
when we ask for God's help,
it seems, after the fact.

CAL FREEMAN

EPISTLE TO DONNE

I don't believe the soul will need these organs
after death. Not the spent kidneys flooding

uric acid into skin, not the sour tongue
with its film like morning fog,

not the heart blown out with nonsense
(few metaphors are anatomically correct),

not the gallbladder like a rotting apple.
I admit the grotesque splendors of nakedness,

but I have trouble imagining these bilge-pumps
and filters surviving the vermiculation

you preached about that first Friday of lent
just weeks before your death

(Izaak Walton says you appeared in the pulpit
that evening as a decayed body and a dying face).

For a decade now I have posed in various versions
of your winding sheet, in thrift store rags, my yellowing

brood mare's teeth jutting out,
bleach splotches on cloth and denim,

grey skin pillowing with toxins. Donne, erstwhile
malt worm, I searched all afternoon

for a blue and white edition of your poems,
through damp boxes of paperbacks

in my garage, dead roaches on odd, sallow pages
like ideograms for sickness. Spiracles globbed

with fipronil and minced-up paper fibers,
begging again your question of dispersal

and reassembly. Poems do not decay like harrowed
congregants; they are disembodied agues at rapture.

PHILIP FRIED

QUANTUM GENESIS

It is like late summer in the void.
If there were grass, its edges would curl
and brown while a deep almost urinous odour
would rise and prevail as mosquitoes and moths
deliriously assaulted a million
screen doors through a night that seemed eternal.

He sits cross-legged in the middle of Nothing
(the mightiest creature who never lived),
about Him a cloud of virtual worlds
that flash into existence and vanish
before He can speak the word. His perfection
is great and unstable and His shame
perfect and vast. Like a swarm of summer
midges, the universes tickle
His cheek and trouble His meditation.

But His only salvation is this beard
of impossible/possible worlds that seethe
out of Nothing seeking His chin, this fuzz
of uncertainty whose filaments curl
and bristle with unnamed tempos and shapes.

He will shelter there with all the unborn
in this ark, this quirky tabernacle,
where He lies down with the virus and lamb,
abiding the quantum genesis.

OWEN GALLAGHER

FEARING THE WRATH

When I discover this book on a hotel bedside table,
   I am reminded of 'Rocky Raccoon', who
   'checked into his room, only to find Gideon's Bible'.

I always ring Reception if I am not greeted
   by this comforter, with its blood-red colour
   and the plea on its cover: 'KINDLY

LEAVE THIS BOOK IN VIEW, THE NEXT GUEST
   MAY NEED IT'. Even for a hard-nosed atheist
   these Boys' Own type stories make good reading.

They often end up in a coat pocket, which might explain
   why one point seven billion have been distributed
   or perhaps God has withdrawn them to be updated, or

they have been used as wedges, or a support for flagging lives.
   I flick this one open to a dog-eared page;
   'And the graves were opened;

and many bodies of the saints which slept arose,
   and came out of the graves after his resurrection,
   and went into the holy city, and appeared unto many'.

Fearing I will be greeted, when I wake for a piss,
   by a roomful of zombies, I place it
   in the drawer and drain the mini-bar.

I recall, as I leave, the scene in which Moses hurled
   God's words at those who departed
   from the heavenly road. I put the book back on display,

the plea on its cover burning like a commandment.

GARY GEDDES

LATE BREAKING NEWS

We're in Wally's Renault, driving
south in Provence, the car radio
harvesting disaster, swaths of it,

and the fields bloody with tulips,
a brash statement stretching
to the low hills of the Luberon.

Later, in the hilltop fortress
with its catapult and trebuchet,
I ask my friend what happened

to monks, to sanctuary, places
where little pain sears the weary
breastbone, where envy's rare

as gourmet meals, where even
the spirited horse, grown
accustomed to lassitude, nudges

the pitchfork's worn handle until
hay falls like manna from the loft,
and where prayers are crafted

in lieu of weapons. Eternity
is long, Pascal has written, so
faith is worth the gamble.

The soul sets sail for a distant
port. Tears mark its departure,
but what marks its arrival?

Planks resound with footsteps,
deep water parts to accommodate
the insistent keel. Wally, amused,

dismisses these speculations,
insists there's romance
in neither monastery nor rose.

Solace, perhaps, though skimpy,
and only in what the moving pen
inscribes or the stiff horsehairs

of the brush render permanent
and lovely, those moments, all
too brief, when the anchor holds

and the sea blooms resplendent
with species of kelp and with the
scrubbed tulip faces of the dead.

DAI GEORGE

THE DRAG CIRCUIT

I never thought that Calvary would flay
the lining from my throat with sour fumes,
or that its sound would be the sound of fire
unfolding through my house. I never thought
that Christ might goad me to a barren strip
outside the city limits, or that love,
unasked-for and impervious, could seize
my hand and clamp it to a steering wheel,
when driving might as well be skinning hares,
so little do I know it, so aghast
am I to feel the pedal at my foot,
the gearstick like a bloody knife at rest.

The course he brings me to is bendless, short;
I couldn't hide if hiding were a choice
that Christ in leathers offered me. His lip
curls. He's Kenickie smiling: will I ride?
Or will I go back to the life that fed
my folly that the cross was only life, not death?

ANDRÁS GEREVICH

CAGE

Half drunk at daybreak, stinking of cigarettes
I slipped into the church, exhausted
after a night spent crushing into parties,
to kneel down before Christ amidst the palms.
A teenager, I loved making such lonely
visits to the empty, noiseless church
so as to send a prayer up for true love.
Because I was secretly in love with my
best friend – torn apart, tortured
with longing for the man in him.
But once I'm through the door today
I can get no further than the grating:
in a shrieking car alarm, the words I cannot find
are like sounding brass, or a tinkling cymbal.

Translated by Christopher Whyte

CLARE GIBBONS

STARRY NIGHT

I understand god
as I understand most

stories: a lonely
child, with an absent

father, a holy ghost
circling through

the house. And the way
it shows is always

different: an eye
peering down the slip

of a kaleidoscope,
sometimes throwing

fields of wheat
onto canvas,

sometimes scribbling
all night, like all my dead.

JOHN GLENDAY

CONCERNING THE ATOMS OF THE SOUL

Someone explained once how the pieces of what we are
fall downwards at the same rate
as the Universe.
The atoms of us, falling towards the centre

of whatever everything is. And we don't see it.
We only sense their slight drag in the lifting hand.
That's what weight is, that communal process of falling.
Furthermore, those atoms carry hooks, like burrs,

hooks catching like hooks, like clinging to like,
that's what keeps us from becoming something else,
and why in early love, we sometimes
feel the tug of the heart snagging against another's heart.

Only the atoms of the soul are perfect spheres
with no means of holding on to the world
or perhaps no need for holding on,
and so they fall through our lives catching

against nothing, like perfect rain,
and in the end, he wrote, mix in that common well of light
at the centre of whatever the suspected
centre is, or might have been.

SUSAN GLICKMAN

JACOB'S LADDER

On the narrow staircase carved into rock at Ein Avdat
tourists pass each other like the angels
on Jacob's ladder; some climbing up, some down.
There's rarely a level path in this land
but if you watch your feet you are as likely to tumble
as if you don't, so just keep going and
someone might take your hand.

The ibex observe us curiously,
their four legs steadier than our two,
and above them the layered cliffs are scarred
with caves emptied of human presence
and bones gnawed by jackals.
The cliffs build towards a sky
that's seen it all before, and will again, and doesn't care.

A few thorny trees bear aromatic fruit: the balm mentioned in the Torah.
Everything here is mentioned in the Torah so that
what once seemed merely myth becomes embodied
folding now into then
and us into them, the ancestors,
who loom higher than the cliffs, their shadows
the shadows of clouds, their memory
the memory of clouds

passing and repassing in the high desert skies
letting fall a rare and welcome rain;
filling the wadis with green.
My heart is full.

My legs tremble with fatigue, but I have
the smell of the Dead Sea in my hair
and a stone for my father's grave
in my pocket.

KEIRAN GODDARD

BROTHER IS BORN
Proverbs 17:17

Map with brittle folds,
shot with sketches,
black circus wheeling through town
confessing every mark –
A cudgeled heap of supple hounds,
A felled ash tree,
A mouth gasping in solitary air.

Pill forced through foil bed,
ill-weathered stone
breaking the skin of water,
addressing the night in whisper –
If I am held,
I am significant,
I am lambent in moonlight.

Final pair on dance-floor,
a grief seen in glances,
the edge of smile,
cracked like hot soil –
I am the frailty of charcoal,
Held in a sculptor's rough hand,
I shiver like dust in the arc of a sunbeam.

Distant canticle,
friendship's steady foot-fall,
a hymn with the strength to rise to,
the sheer truth –
Love's slow,
Purposeful
Healing of wounds.

KIM GOLDBERG

POSSESSED

When the winds came, we lashed ourselves
to fir trees because we knew
what they were and where they stood.
When the waters rose, we packed sandbags
faster than jack rabbits to save the bankrupt farm.
When the thundering maw of canyon fire
clawed the flesh off our bones
we encased our charred skeletons in asbestos
coffins with plexiglas lids
so we wouldn't miss anything.
We wanted it
all – kept all we could. We're still waiting
for that one transcendent
moment, waiting
for you to show us the magic, the secret, the reason
for hanging on.

JOHN GOSSLEE

PORTRAIT OF AN INNER LIFE

a mansion
inside a hovel

an elephant
trapped in a swallow

the claw at the end
of a roar

a frame
without a door

CATHERINE GRAHAM

THERE IS A STIR, ALWAYS

If I hold onto this body the snow will grow inside me
and the winter of my cells will flake
into tiny crystals like six-figured gods,
each arrow tip attempting to make the point of something
as tears flow.

There is a stir, always.

I rise to the cold
to take my place among the fragile stars,
and sleep.

JOHN GREENING

HILDEGARD

I

A harp that bleeds
Heavenwards. A claw
that scratches out
of the blue. Tentacles.

A rubbery gules
reaching a visionary
sea-bed to finger
the face of an anchoress

who has fixed her eyes
on the leering of her
opposite, poking
his tonsure through cobalt

and watching her supple
movements, ready with
his vellum as she touches
the stylus to her wax

and it almost looks
like a hand-held device
though it swells like a buoyancy
aid from a Rhine cruise.

Invisibly, her toes
are twinkling towards
the scarlet footstool,
its cloven hooves.

II

Taste this Bavarian smoked and now this quark.
Coagulation separates light from dark
into a press of cherub cheesewrights. In their ark,
no rising above the Heaven-set plimsoll-mark,

no herding. But curds and whey. Dominions, thrones,
archangels. And angels dreaming of full moons,
seraphic maturity. Labouring ranks of nuns
in Hildegard's creamery, laying stones.

III

Forty years in one place is long enough
to learn the meaning of peace and thirty
to teach the remorselessness

of war. She moves mountains. To Bingen
where the great gorge begins and although
a salt road is preserved,

the singing of railway lines is the hymn
scheduled today at Rupertsberg since men
dynamited the remains

of her monastery the same year the remains
of her spine, skull and choir cap were first
carried in procession.

IV

Other foundations have been blasted too, blown out
and lost over the Pacific, angel regressing to finch,
then to something demonic, supersonic, or satellite-bearing.

How many revolutions since the English Pope? Since Barbarossa?
Between crusades against a crescent and those on moon dust?
From when life expectancy was what you expected after death?

To evolve. While we in a whirlpool – barges, goods trains,
passenger planes and glazed families – go on revolving.
Then nothing, nothing when it's all gone. The silent,

unaltered rails, herbs on the road, and every trail
vaporised to virgin blue. The Rhine forests are dying
for us to burn or pulp. My daughters have taken their bite

of the Apple. My wife reads about apparitions at Versailles.
My sister, I search for illuminations in your *Scivias*:
the great dark star, the cosmic egg, God's wheel.

NICKI GRIFFIN

INCANTATION FOR A GODDESS

Hold the night open.
Decipher the words
made by skeletal trees
against the never-dark sky.

Speak the name you read there
so you are not afraid,
take her hand and let it lead you
down the long valley.

Do not skirt the forest's depth
but plunge to the place
of unhurried light.
Overturn the lichened stone.

Do not step back from
those that squirm and crawl.
The new-lit spot will clear.
Mark well what you find there.

JAMES GRINWIS

SCULPTURE OF ST. FRANCIS HOISTING THE CROSS WITH A WOLF ON IT

For Veracruzana, Northampton, MA

This is just so ridiculously beautiful. I love the wolf.
I love the cross. I love St. Francis. A sculpture from Mexico.
When the wolves were eating so many of the sheep.
And St. Francis is hoisting this lovely canine on his cross.
He is trying to hold it up, his knees are buckling,
but he is holding up the cross with the wolf on the crossbar.
Because he loves the wolf, he loves animals, he
knows the route through despair is being a saint.
A crossbar is a thing on a bike, too. It helps you steer.
A crosscheck is something in hockey, when one player
rams into another player with his stick which makes his body
in the shape of the cross. The wolf will be a wolf.
A sheep will be a sheep. It is said that sometimes a lion
lies down with a sheep, that they are friends. It seems
they have secret messages to each other through the quietude
of being a lion and sheep. When you hear two goats smashing
their heads into each other it is sort of like the clap
you make when you call your dog. Life is so lovely and beautiful,
the connections. It happens mostly when you are sad,
and lonely, when you are a wolf, in need of a saint
to lift you and hold you aloft.

VONA GROARKE

GHOST POEM

Crowded at my window tonight, your ghosts
will have nothing to speak of but us
though the long grass leading to my door
is parted neither by you, leaving

nor by you, coming here. The same ghosts
keep in with my blood, the way
a small name says itself, over
and over, so one minute is cavernous

compared to the next, and I cannot locate
words enough to tell you your wrist
on my breast had the same two sounds to it.
You are a sky over narrow water

and the ghosts at my window
are a full day until I shed their loss.
I want to tell you all their bone-white,
straight-line prophecies

but the thought of you, this very night,
is your veins in silverpoint mapped
on my skin, your will on mine
that I made up and lived inside, as real

and I find I cannot speak of love
or any of its wind-torn ghosts to you
who promised warm sheets and a candle, lit,
but promised me in words.

PHILIP GROSS

MATTINS

And what if (this
   was the sore stiff body
      speaking; this was three a.m.)
       it was all a mistake;

if it wasn't the cool
   and constant soul God loved
      but me?

(This was dark; this was the Mattins

     of the body,
      moving in its slippers
    through the cloisters of itself
to its offices.) Not

     me eternal, resurrected,
   made thirty again, nor
weighted down with grave goods
but this – me as is, as am

in passing.
   If this rusty high C
     of sciatica, low
      chime of heartburn

was the sympathetic quiver
   on my nerve strings
     of the choir

of angels? If *this* was theology:
... imagine it. (This was the wince
   of the floorboard on the landing,
     the half-unwilling almost-
human timbre of the bathroom hinge.)

The body, shrugged clean

of the tricks and self-
   deceptions of the mind,
     stepping out of (or into) itself
like the pool of Siloam,

in a dog-shake of spray-drips of light...

The body made new –
   not *young*... Not the body
     in general but this one
in time, with its stuttering-out like stars

of brain cells, with what may be the hum

of a home in its ears, pipes clicking,
   an appliance shuddering to rest,
     the bare skin chilling, and
each breath a little of its warmth
dispersed... Body washed in the blood

of its own veins, baptised
   from within with the kiss
     and the commerce of oxygen,
of carbon, of their conversation. If it was *this*

God loved, if the secret got out...
                      well, what then?

DAVID GRUBB

THE BLUE CATHEDRAL
for Rupert Loydell

One

We will try to get here when the world is ending;
some people have reached the end already which is
why they are hanging up their prayers in the almost
silence and letting the blue burn them and when they
do speak it is in another language which we do not know.
They do not see the priests or the tourists or the bookshop;
they are searching for angels and white doves and messages;
they are hungry for wonders and radiance and the flecks of
everlasting wisdom that they know still exist between pillars
and densities and what the windows let in between narratives
of suffering and splendour and burnished tapestries of light.
The light is always blue here. When we enter it is always a
beginning. We move into the blue and sometimes I wonder
if we ever come out again. Some of the people here carry
the dead in their arms. They no longer need birdsong to
make this world real. I can see the outlines of some of them
entering the stone of the dome, these blue transformations.

Two

And if the God is not here? And if what we bring here falls down,
these ornaments and incantations and ideas of beholding, these small
necessities and declarations and garments of the soul; what then?
And if the God is a tiger or a bird, if the God is a silence or a song,
if God is a colour, if God is rivers, if God is deep earth, if God is a wind,
if God is the middle of the riddle, if God is the everlasting story, if God
is the creature that we have created because there has to be a creature;

what then? The blue cathedral submits. The blue cathedral makes a miracle of being. The blue cathedral holds us in its eye and we travel here to meet whatever we have been. And we wait like stained glass people who belong to a scene where a miracle has taken its place; the blind man rides his bike, the dead man raises another glass of wine and the children who were slaughtered speak quietly to a unicorn.

EVE GRUBIN

WHO RELEASES THE BOUND, WHO STRAIGHTENS THE BENT

Underneath this missing another
missing: familiar, unremembered. The mirror

stares at my bed, the bookshelves have nothing
to say to me. This longing

hangs heavy, the taste of it
filling the back of my mouth. Black rain
suspends past shut windows and brick.

A breathing in my dress
when I bend to the drawer for a shirt,

when air slides through the slit under the unopened window
and reaches my naked elbow.

Let the longing lift north attaching
to the next rung and the next until I speak

translucent, seeable
give me quick
transparent noticing, close.

What is real?
Thin bones glow
in my ankle, my rib,
a hand rests above the roof
of my house, above the oak beside it.
Blessed are you who releases the bound.

Ache in my unwinged thighs, my belly an unblessed field.
Who straightens the bent.
Your many names are stuck in my throat.

KATIA GRUBISIC

LADDER TO THE MIDDLE

The ladder, perplexed at the utility that calls it out into the disquiet
of the work lights on the empty stage, draws down

the corners of its mouth, stops with hands on its hips, feet apart.
But for an invitation, it could dispense invaluable advice, rules

for the way we move: to be edgy, use your elbows more. It dies
a little in indecision and prefers, artlessly, to leave the fold and fall

to others. In any case, there's really no changing its mind.
Once the climb and tinkering are complete – and the descent too,

it wouldn't do to leave a man marooned
in mid-air – it will be relegated to toy boxes, dreams

and the forms of angels. It knows about luck,
shabby English stockings, obsolete elevators. But it stands

for the victory of geometry, and only wants
to get closer to god, to bring us there.

KATHRYN HAMANN

BIBLES – HIS AND HERS

The CRC Handbook of Chemistry and Physics,
88th Edition
                is a resistance constant
that can hold any door
                from slipping
into lock

Winter gathering within flocked walls...
There was a summer promise but no
one has brought the paper or coal;
no match has started smoke
symbols of heat

A chill raised to the factor of age
– frost to him but at least away
from the packing his belongings
for yet another removal   I
ever restless till he is put to rest
in the Dementia Ward
High Care

To lie in bed at night and snuggle
down in the plump comfort: *He is safe...*
never allowed to escape the friction
of my care

But this finally arrived tome necessitates
his strength added to mine to lift it
to the table... Chortles sequence
into unison...

I can open this book...

a language closed to me
but we have the index
and this I read aloud…
His comments well spaced
on its usefulness
allow a little breathing…
a straying into the biological
sciences… and I can sigh
wistful truth: *How useful*
this would have been…

We have both worked in labs…
He at the apex /
Me plating bacteria for…
there is a complement here…
He with his Bible…
Mine – with its narratives   metaphors
contradictions   illogicalities
its chequered history
frequent brutalities –
and a language like
the language
                    of affection
closed to him

And yet as coated arms rub one
against other in our reading
there is a coaxing
of a small flame
now flaring through figures
symbols… until he is as old – a new
explorer of the mind's
territory

I remember how the daily paper
would emerge from his hands
embroidered with formulae
He would growl how
Einstein lost time
trying to pin God
within the vastness
of subatomic emptiness
(where a spinning electron
denies certainty) and
yet here in these pages
he ushers his servant some-
where she could never
go alone

We repeat and repeat
the experiment finding ease
in the index's unflinching
progression and from super
saturation – crystals
of Wisdom
            through their planes
time curves on its own
axis
       and Joy
is shown to be
       the only constant
with the power that can
balance the equation of
he and I

TOM HAMILL

THE ONE DEEPNESS

As this 21st century unfolds,
A blessed truth's beginning to tap on the window:
'Child-of-God! It's time you realised
How many serious deepnesses you're plunged-into
But not, or hardly at all, the one-deepness
That brings totality-of-healing for self-and-all ...'
Perhaps I'm so-emplunged I never hear,
Or so bemused I think it's a wee hawk ...
'Cos truths don't tap like that on glass,
But arrange authoritative mouths, like emperors-and-popes ...
God's-truth, that's what I've always heard,
Comes from the throne, never a tap on the window ...

Then, out of the blue, an eagle hovered,
Someone hinting, now it's time for action!
Not the insistent hawk, nor the crooning dove,
But Yahweh'sBird-that-Carried-The-Folk-with-Love
From Darkness, on TheBreath-of-Chokmah-The-Wise ...

Yes! The ClingingDeepness-of-Self-Obsession!
Yes! TheDeepeningDeepness-of-Self-Delusion!
Yes! The SoaringDeepness-of-Fancy'sFear!
Yes! The ShallowDeepness! TheLetter-that-Kills!
Yes! TheBitingDeepness-of-MordantGuilt!
Yes! The UnreachableDeepness-of-LoveBetrayed!
Yes! TheImmanentDeepness-of-TheFamily-Tree!
Yes! TheCircumambientDeepness-of-Apathy!
But, Yes! The NurturingDeepness-of-TheMaster'sNarratives!
But, Yes! ThatDeepness-of-The Breath'sEnthusement!

And What action does Yahweh's Eagle urge?
This! 'Plunge-in-TheOnlyDeepness-of-Worth!
Awake and Realise and Manifest!
Follow-The-Master-into-The-Pool-of-TheBreath!
And There-Embrace-TheMystery-of-YourOwnTrueSelf…'

But, maybe the Eagle's just Having-a-Squawk …

LUKE HANKINS

EQUAL AND OPPOSITE

Looking at the sky, the word *sky*
comes to mind. The word has a referent –
the sky itself – but the sky itself
has no referent. To live in language
is to anticipate metaphor,
but in this moment I sense the void
upon which, all these years, I have built
my house of words.
Only come with me
to the precipice where I peer in terror,
I pray, grasping at words
that offer no resistance
like feathers snatched from the air,
like ropes not tied to anything.
I plunge through the world
that is no language
praying (in my language)
to the absent Referent,
the force equal and opposite
to the void, the grip that can
(I pray) suspend my fall
so that I can hang
in what the sky means.

MORGAN HARLOW

CIVILIZATION

hinges on this
    the cutting of onions
  bay leaves
salt

 a burning bush
  be explained
     by drought
 lightning or autumn
    fire

ALEX HARTLEY

THE ANNUNCIATION
After da Vinci

Mary, you are like an opening flower.
I cannot come too near for fear that you
will rupture – first your hand splitting in two,
your clothes unpeeling, falling in a shower

of petals, your skin opening to display
something white and whole, a bright perfection
that is the archangel. I am the reflection
of within-you. A body is only clay.

Mary, I have come to close the chain,
to fill the room, to seal the gaping skin.
I step inside you now. Step through the glass
into your womb. And so it comes to pass
a child will be born. And into him
all people will step at the end of pain.

TERRANCE HAYES

THE CARPENTER ANT

It was when or because she became two kinds
of mad, both a feral nail biting into a plank
and a deranged screw cranking into a wood beam,
the aunt – I shouldn't say her name,

went at the fullest hour of the night,
the moon there like an unflowered bulb
in a darkness like mud, or covered in darkness
as a bulb or skull is covered in mud,

the small brown aunt who, before she went mad,
taught herself to carpenter and unhinged,
in her madness, the walls she claimed
were bugged with a tiny red-eyed device

planted by the State or Satan's agents, ghosts
of atheists, her foes, or worse, the walls
were full of the bugs she believed crawled
from her former son-in-law's crooked mouth,

the aunt, who knows as all creatures know,
you have to be rooted in something tangible
as wood if you wish to dream in peace,
took her hammer with its claw like a mandible

to her own handmade housing humming,
'*I don't know why God keeps blessing me,*'
softly madly, and I understood, I was with her
when the pallbearers carried a box

made of mahogany from her church to a hearse
to a hole in the earth, it made me think
of the carpenter ant who carries within its blood
an evolved self-destructive property, and on its face

mandibles twice the size of its body,
and can carry on its back, as I have seen on tv,
a rotted bird or branch great distances
to wherever the queen is buried – Kingdom:

Animalia, Phylum*: Arthropoda,* Tribe*: Camponotini,*
the species that lives on wood is, like mud, rain,
and time, the carpenter's enemy, yes,
but I would love to devour the house I live in

until it is a permanent part of me,
I would love to shape, as Perumthachan,
the master sculptor, carpenter and architect
of India is said to have shaped, a beautiful tree

into the coffin in which I am to be buried,
I know whatever we place in a coffin, the coffin
remains empty, I know nothing buried is buried,
I don't know why God keeps blessing me,

I don't know why God keeps blessing me.

KEVIN HIGGINS

A LETTER GOD SHOULD BE AFRAID TO OPEN
after Nanci Griffith

I have read your application with interest.
From your astronaut distance
the world may look blue and green. Yes.
The five wide oceans and Himalayas,
you spent Tuesday and Wednesday
perfecting, cannot but impress.

Down here, all my worst things line up
at the end of the driveway, like salesmen
in suits that died years ago,
and begin their approach.

Idiocy rings the doorbell.
The tongue flapping around in his head
enhanced by the slight smell of *Jeyes Fluid*.
I ask to speak to his supervisor,
but the number he writes down for me
is my own.

Unforeseen consequences
let themselves in the side door,
patio window unnoticed.
The house fills up with
outcomes no one intended
and no insurance policy can fix.
From here the world is mostly
old clothes, damp bath mats. Death
is at the kitchen table

and tells me: *whatever happens,*
it's the same dark place I'm going to
and I won't meet anybody there.

Thank you for your interest.
But even if you existed,
you wouldn't be up to the job.
        Yours etc.

NORBERT HIRSCHHORN

AVINU MALKEYNU

'Avinu Malkeynu', 'Our Father Our King', is sung during the High Holy days: Rosh Hashanah, the New Year, and Yom Kippur, the Day of Atonement.

Answer me.
A blind minstrel, wandering the wilderness descends
a valley with his
kitara made of boxwood, wanting
for consolation. Let the great
horned owl keep its eyes perpetually
open, an emptiness staring
in, an emptiness staring out.
Answer me.
For I am wanting. Scraps
of paper in my pocket: Eggs,
milk, honey, immortality, kiss
the kids. I am
good enough. I have
no life. Live it well. No answer
comes. I mustn't ask. No
lists, pleas, promises, no apologies. The ram's horn
sounds a Jericho blast. Save me.

LINDSEY HOLLAND

QUANTUM BEACH

We stand at the tideline. Today it's almost up
to the dunes, a rope of starfish carried down
from an ocean where neither charm
nor prayer work. You say it's strange
we often strain for a prospect at the top
of hills and towers when at the bottom

these cells, villi, mouths come up
in chaotic splutter, pulse, sink down.
I don't know what to think. Your charm
is something more than words. Your eyes' strange
green is blood but your hooded top
is impossible turquoise chemical. The bottom

of the dune, its sly foot, shuffles up
an inch a year to the marsh then down
to fishing shacks that decay into charm,
but there's little proof of movement, no strange,
uncanny sneak or slip. From the top
the sea is whole and the sand at the bottom

a single skin. Its pores gather up
into chapels and pyramids. Further down
the tideline's bracelet, charm by charm,
is barely visible, twisted, strange.
I must look beyond. We rush for the top
while miracle curls into shell at the bottom.

ANNETTE HOLLANDER

GOD COMES TO ME AT 6 P.M.

God comes to me at 6 P.M. That's when
brick walls begin to glow, when golden light
flows down old theatre posters and graffiti
beckon, awesome. See my city shine!
People in busy streets carry their glow
on pinstripe suits, not knowing they are blessed.

I do nothing to deserve my being blessed
an hour before sunset. Even when
dark thoughts pollute, silences can glow.
Familiar dirty avenues delight,
sport elevated subway cars that shine,
decorated with the best graffiti.

I'm not a person who would make graffiti
or spend much time thinking about being blessed;
I'm always stunned when streets begin to shine,
sidewalks implode. I can't believe it when
I feel that Presence in the spreading light.
I stare, not seeing my own body's glow.

Once I saw fields and a farmhouse glow
(initials cut in bark are trees' graffiti).
Watching the hedgerow in the evening light
– even barbed wire fences can be blessed –
I could not say what happened to me when
I was only eight and saw the shine

the first time, sitting down, feeling the shine
embrace the meadow while the sky-clouds glow
surrounded ponies. Blackbirds, flocking, when
the sky grew red, drew lines of wild graffiti.
I never thought, then, about words like 'blessed'.
I only knew I was part of the light

that quivered everywhere. This moving light,
fifty years later, strikes me with its shine
abruptly as the first day I was blessed
with losing me. I hope you've seen this glow
even if you've never heard graffiti
say, 'Now!' Open your eyes. I told you when.

And in that hour of glow, when flaming light
shines on our world, on cow dung or graffiti,
anyone, anywhere who sees it can be blessed.

PAUL HOOVER

WHAT THE CUTTING LOCUST LEAVES
Your old men shall dream dreams

        Be not afraid,
for the Lord will do great things.
He will assemble the innocent
and breathe upon the heathen.
He will mount a banquet
for thieves and their victims,
for the harlot and her loved ones,
the schemer and his reasons.
The voice will find its face,
body find its rhyme
and mind its perfect season.
If the fields are wasted,
faith will double their grain;
hope will make ready
the living and the dead.
For what a god leaves,
the night will carry away;
and what the night carries,
the eyes will transform,
and what the eye transforms,
the heart will pay in tender.
Though a fire may burn behind me
and another approach straight ahead,
the door of the forest will open;
the eye of the leaf will weep;
spring will cut the throat of fall,
and winter will be our Eden.
        Therefore, be not afraid,
for generous god overflows his banks
and leaps like myth from the fire.

Where, he asks, do they ever grow young?
When is time on time?
For the years run like horses
to the brink and never turn.
And the old men dream their dreams
of the honey-pot and the bee,
the drowning song and the song
of the office terriers, Terence,
Tony, and Tom. But the sons
and daughters of sons will prophesy
what the swarming locust sings
of the cutting locust's remains,
whereupon history turns.
There are men who turn to gods
and fall from highest spire,
and gods that wither away,
leaving a man newborn.
The handsomest god dies first,
eyeing his brides and grooms,
for the day of his fate is so fine,
so steadfast in its desires,
how shall he live through it?

SHERRY HOROWITZ

IN THE BEGINNING

Though He is uncontainable, unimaginable —
Imagine eternity is an exposé rendering love obsolete:
Imagine knowing everything without a doubt.

Imagine —
Restraint and limit facilitate mystery —

What do we know when we know everything?
What would be left to say?

What you don't know: A perimeter, containment,
Arms gathering you in closer —

Though I say I love you forever, we both know
It is only for as long as we live —

We live, one minute after another in uncertainty,
By way of clumsiness and greed.

By way of wanting more than what holds us together.
Just a little more…
When you have everything, what is left to give?

The soul left empty-handed knew this —
Imagine God answering:
Because I love you I give you the world.

FANNY HOWE

AT IFFLEY LOCK

Homeless and
leaning over,
suddenly older: 'Without you, God,
I can't continue'.

Who said that?

You hoist the bag and walk
to search for one book.
One book only!

Up Iffley Turn to the Hawkwell and Tree Inns
and down over a lock
into an extended filthy river
through the Thames Valley
and across a meadow into town:
two fats, one fishing and one man on a bike
swerving through Cotswold cow pads

You ask each one:
'Do you know the fastest way
to City Centre?'

No, yes, no!
Circle Magdalen college, and the mall, the High,
Broad Street, PO and Headington Hill,
Brookside and Christ Church,
cross big pavement stones and cobbles
to Holywell

and down North Parade, Maison Blanc, Browns,
the Phoenix Cinema on Walton Street
where you can bring your wine into the film.

So on to the asbestos,
white dusty condiments, Pret a Manger,
T.S. Eliot, smelly markets, buskers
on a harp, Philip Larkin's *Girl in Winter*,
and a xylophone, buses and bicycles.
Red-faced riotously quiet British...
Earl green carpets and rotten wood frames,
lavender, and buttery daisies,
flagelot beams, bar food, the stink of perfumes
over toilets, Blackwell's Books has none of him,
St. Philips will.
What name are you looking for?
Thomas Merton.

(There are so many mental perches
and Abbot Patrick, in his cassock, stands high above
and smiles and says: You see? It's all right
the church is in ruins.)

The devil runs the world was Adam's discovery
so now it's time to pray
to Blake's engravings of the double bind.
I made this fruit for you. Don't eat it!

At St. Philips you ask:
'Do you carry *The Seven Storey Mountain*?'

No.
Everything you see is finished.
Even the ground underfoot and ahead.
The paper and its ink – over.
The book is out of print.

ANTHONY HOWELL

THE TEMPTATION

I
Wilderness

He was led by a voice in a stream, until the stream vanished
And there was only the voice, leading him by the ear,
Until he came to the wilderness, then the voice chuckled
And evaporated among the chuckles of stunted reptiles.
Sky cradled no cloud. The bushes would not burn.
Once, a solitary Phoenix hazed on a far rock,
But disintegrated immediately into a mound of ashes.
Each day, the blabbermouthed baker paid him a visit, bearing
Stone pellets to his marble hutch, grinning, unlatching the jaw,
Saying, 'Scones. They are scones. Taste one'.
But he knew them to be stones or dung;
Camel dung mixed with the sands or petrified by the ages.
Perservering, pestering, it shoved them under his nose,
'Smell bread', gibbered the tempter, 'smell'.
The smell very closely resembled new baked bread,
But might have been Brimstone. 'Where is your faith?
To the faithful this tastes like bread',
It taunted him, gnawing the stones. Forty days,
Forty years concentrated in as many days,
And not by bread, by bread alone shall he survive them.
Must learn to survive on the leftovers;
Berry and husk when Blabbermouth takes himself off.
Religion's tit-bits, waters of reflection;
De l'eau non potable, nail-filings, scraps in The Lord's garden.
At dawn, dew rises like yeast.
He crawled out to lick the bewildered stones.
Quails plump themselves down and will not budge;
Sabbath days, a roasted quail strutted across the threshold.

His hunger stemmed from an appetite indifferent to emptiness.
He had long entertained the suspicion, 'I AM THY BREAD'.

II
Pinnacle

Out of the whispering gallery by a coil of steps,
At the top of which blazed the roof. Thence, by a ladder
With as many rungs missing as Methusalah lacked teeth,
To the pinnacle, where his colleague importuned him.
'Leap. The pinnacle you stand on is His fortress;
And He is your refuge and your fortress, leap.
He will deliver you from the snare of the fowler,
If not from the noisome pestilence I personify.
Let no one call the tempter an agnostic,
Look down. There are the ancient wings spread waiting.
Where is your faith?' He had no need of faith.
An opened map, his short life lay below him:
Rama, where tin soldiers spitted pink cicadas;
Close at hand, the hollow hill, the weekly scaffold.
Falling, he would plummet through the cages of the doves.
'I have no need of faith, which I personify.
Would you tempt me as you tempted me in Massah?
Wound that rock, my blood will swamp this city,
Drench the world it draws about it for a cloak.
A generation of stars will shine more damply. Death
Is a form of madness. There is no sin greater than to tempt
The Lord thy God with such lascivious madness, dream
Called death. The eternal city with its long dunes'.
And he remained on the pinnacle, deliberating this
For as long as a city's braziers may bewitch the shepherd.
With the devil beside him, he gazed on the deep sea;
Whether to pitch himself again into that long instant.
The breast quietening the mouth in Galilee.

III
Kingdoms

It was late afternoon. They were arguing in the gardens;
Their wits made sharp by citrons in the shade.
Then they were moving, silently, mounting the terraces;
Señor in the lead, switching at grapes with his cane.
Almost by accident, they came to the high place.
Cities were suspended in the haze below them
Like Portugese Men-of-War, pendulous with gardens.
The snail paced river left a silver trail.
Even at this height, a stench of fats, issuing
From the scent-works, was formidable. Then the smokes
Were halted in their rising. And Señor
Fingered each kingdom as he might his beads.
He described the holiness of the waters –
What beliefs were to be had, and at which wells;
And the profits annually from their bottling.
How every parish boasted at least one shrine per toll-gate;
How each cathedral disgorged a carpet like a tongue
To lap up obeisant ladies and their lords.
Livings were comfy. Ought he not to be ordained?
He smiled. 'I had not thought you so unsubtle
As to imagine steeplehouses tempt me.
The motionless kingdom suffers no promotions,
Mine nor yours. Those Hierarchies
Make such a poor investment;
I confess my preoccupations are with this world.
Angel, get thee behind me'.
With this profanity, he left Señor,
And went down alone among the soughing groves.
A dark form losing its figure in the darker Cedars,
While the tempter remained on high, reciting his credo.

SUSAN IOANNOU

FAR NORTH

Far north,
when blue curves closer
as if to cup the earth

between outcrop
and pine's needled spaces
mind can almost touch a Presence

until past dusk
the darkness crystallises
– one after one – such stars!

A sprinkle, scatterings, multitudes
layering thicker and thicker
than any imagined vision

glittering from immensities of black,
beyond and beyond
and beyond

– how can a single Spirit
watch over it all?

SALLY ITO

FOR THE ATHEIST

There will be no casting of aspersions —
for the heart is a primitive organ
and it is too easy to hate —

O wicked worker of iniquity,
mine enemy, deceiver, maker of lies.

No. Instead, a marveling at the tempered calm
of this believer of nothing
who does not fall prey to the silly, fool emotions
a god is said to inspire:

Thank you! Thank you!

Praise You!

O help! Help!

Ashamed of the dumbstruck wonder
that is my soul's need, sheepish in the tent
of faith, my glimpse of the
One who believeth not
is of admiration.

Still, this is not an ode
but rather reluctant praise
from the plucked gut of a wounded animal
for the one not yet struck,
bounding away, in leaps and strides
into the dark hills beyond the hunter's gaze —
praise for the creature, whole and without blemish,
praise for the one who needs no sacrifice.

CHRISTOPHER JACKSON

WOOD-VOICE
(for Robert Peake)

after 'The Dream of the Rood'

It was years ago. I was felled —
upended, bundled along the clearing,
up a dead ridge and down a verge
where an incision of light, like a nail,
suggested hysteria to swans.
They chased each other round the pond.
I expected to be a gallows for bandits.
I was shouldered to a hilltop,
and wedged into the cool clay.
He came to me almost quickly,
and fastened himself to my stoicism.
I accepted a human weight;
the nails were a disaster for me too.
I looked down on my brothers:
the valleyed, emerald or lemon
with superfluity of leaf.
They had no morbid eminence,
and were not carpentered
to any shape of suffering:
without death there is no narrative.
He was riding the jeers underneath,
announcing another knowledge
than the physics of things:
his meekness implied that
he was ruled by a jurisdiction
distinct from Caesar's vanity,
or Herod's architecture.
I was received into their mockery.
Blood seeped into my rings;

storm was the clothing on our backs.
After the insane hour had arrived
and the mother was weeping,
and the friends were fearful,
wondering if they'd still know
how to philosophise,
or even how to praise the strange
and governed universe,
they tore out the offensive nails,
and the body went limp,
confessing all difficulty.
The loincloth billowed like leaf.
Thunder was large in all things.
I emitted the sodden complaint
of rained-upon wood.

MARK JARMAN

THAT TEENAGER WHO PROWLED OLD BOOKS

That teenager who prowled old books to find
Any argument with a whiff of the Holy Ghost –
I meet him again in his marginalia,
Which ignored the common sweat and stink and marked
Those passages that confirmed what he was hunting.
There was the milk white hart of evidence.
There was the hound of heaven, italicized bold,
Like an angry footnote chasing it off the page.
And there were the hunters, in pursuit themselves –
Plato, Lucretius, Virgil, Marcus Aurelius –
Who did not know he knew what they were after.
And so he missed a lot, all of it human,
Even while scribbling black and blue Eurekas!,
Bleeding through pages backwards, to note irrelevance.
It was all about something else, which he didn't see,
As philosophers mounted their lovers from behind
And felt their limbs go dead from the toes upward,
And poets kissed a mouth that fastened tight
And locked tongues and tried to catch their breath.

TROY JOLLIMORE

TOM THOMSON IN DOUBT

The plan fell through. Nor would he (that is, He)
admit that there had even been a plan.
He didn't sign his work. Remained He mum.
Still did the people speculate. The prea-

chers say: 'Have faith. He's up there'. They contest:
'I talked to Him last night. He just was here.
He stepped out for a minute'. People bought it
(some) or made as if they did (the rest.)

But Tom could not. *If He is*, puzzled he,
He must not want *us to believe*. He knew,
like any good executive in chief,
that Plausible Deniability

matters above all else. *That settles it, then:*
nothing is settled. Or will be. Amen.

TESS JOLLY

PRAYER

If I prayed at all it wasn't when I thought you were dying,
when children and dogs oozed from pavements
to gawp at you: a falang with shrivelled limbs and jaw
hanging, eyes dragged deep in their sockets.
I shooed them away and sat beside you trying not to look,
or remember nurses laughing at the clinic
because it was a day after the full-moon party
and they thought you were high. They refused a blood-test
on a public holiday with no doctors in until morning.
It was mid-afternoon and you muttered and raved.
I didn't know what was wrong but I knew you wouldn't last
another night like this, so I signed the forms
and we left, we struggled like drunkards to the jetty – your legs
buckling under every other step. I held your head
to stop you from choking and waited for the boat
to the other island, the one with a hospital and doctors
who pushed me aside, wired you to monitors and drips
then pumped you and pumped you with insulin for six hours.
If I prayed at all – and I doubt I did because we'd stopped
believing in God – there was a moment in the sudden
lull of it all, steady hum of geckos, shuttle of your breath,
when I walked to the window, looked out at palm trees
and the first drops of rain that would pour all week,
listened to water wash the beach with sea-birds' cries,
then looked up at the stars and flush of moonlight
on a shimmering, darkening tide. If I prayed at all
it was then, and I whispered, in case you woke and heard.

JILL JONES

BIG FLOWER

I haven't had that dream again
night visitor death and the big flower
I did not even die but rose
through the strata, plains of clouds
beams, quivers, satellites, walkers
to the place the moon might be
somewhere around earth but
just a slip eastward, northward
in the shaky sky beyond the sky
where the birds come from where
they all talked on the ground
before trees looked like trees
when I was young I dreamed of
tunnels, of walking passages
of hydrangeas to blue-green death
but I did not die I flew
I thought this proved something
or would make me content with
the way things were, wearisome
worthwhile or perhaps just wonky.
Death knows me, the moon knows
me, I see that smile on the birds
that know me in the tree
to the northeast, me, their bright
bodies the least of my preparations.

LOIS P. JONES

THE LANDSCAPE OF FLIGHT
for Susan Rogers

Once you have tasted flight you will walk the earth with your eyes turned skywards, for there
you have been and there you will long to return. – Leonardo da Vinci

1. Bone

A hawk landed in your cradle and pressed
its tail feathers into your mouth

explaining your taste for flight, a need
to pull the buzzard apart with slender fingers

looking for secrets in the articulated wings. There,
in the late hours the scent of wax burns your nostrils

as you pry the codex, cracking the contours, drawing
the downy tufts apart. You note the breast bone

shaped like a keel, lay out each pearled shaft
until it reclaims its shape. Candles come

and go like sylphs, casting shadows
on the freshly inked sketches.

When you finally walk the corridor to your room,
feathers fall around you to the tiled floors, lodge

in your velvet robes and pillows. Sleep arrives
slender as a wing-bone. You dream you are

a black crane flying low across the Arno,
the moon a plume nearly gone.

2. Earth

I've been trying for so long to leave you
I get as far as I can

until gravity pulls me back
maybe my wings are too solid
my breath heavier than salt

bones too dense to lift into the airstream
too warm-blooded to plunge
into the folds of space where nothing
answers my call.

3. Flower

Look at these dogwood blossoms.
Each caught in the act of flying.
Each in pursuit of motion,
white wings bent and touching
in a flock of origami.
They could be cranes adrift
in the impermanence of dying.

Maybe every blossom is another chance
at goodness, the purity of a new life,
a hope to be born into it.

'Flower' after the photograph Kousa Dogwood Blossoms *by Peter Shefler.*

MARY JONES

CREATION

A sudden stillness in a roar of flame
and all is changed, a wondering world is born.
The billowing darkness trembles and is torn
and then continues, nevermore the same;
no longer purposeless, without a name,
but fashioned, formed, inexorably drawn
writhing reluctantly towards the dawn
out of the depths before the earth became.
And in that moment, waking out of sleep
and singing through the silences alone
on wings of flame, rejoicing to be free,
the spirit moves across the empty deep,
and in the void the seeds of time are sown
to bud and blossom to eternity.

OLIVER JONES

LET THERE BE WHATEVER

God said 'let there be light', but it was a sham
or a kind of joke I guess, typical of
his mania for obscurantism.

I know because I've got the goggles out,
flicked the light switch on and off and watched
very closely the dance of the filaments.

I see nothing in there that I did not put in myself.

God said 'let there be light', but I felt very
heavy sitting on a second-hand mattress,
poking at the cheap plaster, watching shadows
jump into life and out of it like hyperactive Lazuri.

Still, I agree that there might be a kind of
God whose orange fingers are curled in
those glowing tungsten threads – but you can't
trust me on this: I find Gods in all sorts
of unlikely places.

Like in the sonic nuance emitted by
a shorn sine wave (that makes me wanna dance)
or in the thrilling and complicated warmth
of an animal's fur (my girl laughing,
my kissing her when it's sunny). In the eyes
of a stranger (fuck! and in a fight!),
in the desperate vibrations of a
tightly packed sphincter (and in all the things
you can't deny – love, pain, nausea, gopher-holing),

in my brother's face when he impersonates
dad and reverses time (I laugh like crazy).

God said 'let there be light' because he knew
that first impressions count. So perhaps there is
a God in that light he's so proud of –
– that soft-focus light in wuxia films
that makes your memory reel in reverse –
– maybe somehow coded in the dispersal
patterns of His radiant solar waves.

Perhaps he's also in the darkness, whose kiss
possesses a thousand implied images,
or in the complex stirrings that wrap my heart
in a coffin of shivers. Perhaps not.

God said 'let there be a firmament', but I
feel as infirm as anyone ever did.
And though there are clusters of starmelt under
our car parks, and our brains emit fields of
the same electromagnetic form
as the sun and the lightbulb, and though
molluscs, DNA and the Milky Way
are bound in the same Fibonacci spiral,
and though time cannot pass because it has
no time to pass in, and though semantic recursions
bind our language in these divinely mysterious
paradoxes, and though people can just
be so sublimely difficult to really know,
between you and me, I gotta confess
it doesn't bug me as much as it used to.

God said a whole lot of things, and appeared
particularly fond of the phrase 'and it was so',
but I prefer 'and so what?'.

As in:

God said   'Let there be lights in the vault of the sky,
            let dry ground appear,
            let the earth put forth grass,
            let the water teem with living creatures,
            let birds fly above the earth,
            let us make mankind in our image'

and so what?

FADY JOUDAH

PROPOSAL

I think of god as a little bird who takes
To staying close to the earth,
The destiny of little wings
To exaggerate the wind
And peck the ground.

I see Haifa
By my father and your father's sea,
The sea with little living in it,
Fished out like a land.

I think of a little song and
How there must be a tree.

I choose the sycamore
I saw split in two
Minaret trunks on the way
To a stone village in a stone-thrower mountain.

Were the villagers wrong to love
Their donkeys and wheat for so long,
To sing to the good stranger
Their departure song?

I think of the tree that is a circle
In a straight line, future and past.
I wait for the wind to send
God down, I become ready for song.

I sing, in a tongue not my own:
We left our shoes behind and fled.
We left our scent in them
Then bled out our soles.
We left our mice and lizards

There in our kitchens and on the walls.
But they crossed the desert after us,
Some found our feet in the sand and slept,
Some homed in on us like pigeons
Then built their towers in a city coffin for us.

I will probably visit you there after Haifa.
A little bird to exaggerate the wind
And lick the salt off the sea of my wings. I think

God reels the earth in when the sky rains
Like fish on a wire.

And the sea, each time it reaches the shore,
Becomes a bird to see of the land
What it otherwise wouldn't.
And the wind through the trees
Is the sea coming home.

ILYA KAMINSKY

AUTHOR'S PRAYER

If I speak for the dead, I must leave
this animal of my body,

I must write the same poem over and over,
for an empty page is the white flag of their surrender.

If I speak for them, I must walk on the edge
of myself, I must live as a blind man

who runs through rooms without
touching the furniture.

Yes, I live. I can cross the streets asking 'What year is it?'
I can dance in my sleep and laugh

in front of the mirror.
Even sleep is a prayer, Lord,

I will praise your madness, and
in a language not mine, speak

of music that wakes us, music
in which we move. For whatever I say

is a kind of petition, and the darkest
days must I praise.

BRIGIT PEGEEN KELLY

SONG

Listen: there was a goat's head hanging by ropes in a tree.
All night it hung there and sang. And those who heard it
Felt a hurt in their hearts and thought they were hearing
The song of a night bird. They sat up in their beds, and then
They lay back down again. In the night wind, the goat's head
Swayed back and forth, and from far off it shone faintly
The way the moonlight shone on the train tracks miles away
Beside which the goat's headless body lay. Some boys
Had hacked its head off. It was harder work than they had imagined.
The goat cried like a man and struggled hard. But they
Finished the job. They hung the bleeding head by the school
And then ran off into the darkness that seems to hide everything.
The head hung in the tree. The body lay by the tracks.
The head called to the body. The body to the head.
They missed each other. The missing grew large between them,
Until it pulled the heart right out of the body, until
The drawn heart flew toward the head, flew as a bird flies
Back to its cage and the familiar perch from which it trills.
Then the heart sang in the head, softly at first and then louder,
Sang long and low until the morning light came up over
The school and over the tree, and then the singing stopped...
The goat had belonged to a small girl. She named
The goat Broken Thorn Sweet Blackberry, named it after
The night's bush of stars, because the goat's silky hair
Was dark as well water, because it had eyes like wild fruit.
The girl lived near a high railroad track. At night
She heard the trains passing, the sweet sound of the train's horn
Pouring softly over her bed, and each morning she woke
To give the bleating goat his pail of warm milk. She sang
Him songs about girls with ropes and cooks in boats.
She brushed him with a stiff brush. She dreamed daily

That he grew bigger, and he did. She thought her dreaming
Made it so. But one night the girl didn't hear the train's horn,
And the next morning she woke to an empty yard. The goat
Was gone. Everything looked strange. It was as if a storm
Had passed through while she slept, wind and stones, rain
Stripping the branches of fruit. She knew that someone
Had stolen the goat and that he had come to harm. She called
To him. All morning and into the afternoon, she called
And called. She walked and walked. In her chest a bad feeling
Like the feeling of the stones gouging the soft undersides
Of her bare feet. Then somebody found the goat's body
By the high tracks, the flies already filling their soft bottles
At the goat's torn neck. Then somebody found the head
Hanging in a tree by the school. They hurried to take
These things away so that the girl would not see them.
They hurried to raise money to buy the girl another goat.
They hurried to find the boys who had done this, to hear
Them say it was a joke, a joke, it was nothing but a joke...
But listen: here is the point. The boys thought to have
Their fun and be done with it. It was harder work than they
Had imagined, this silly sacrifice, but they finished the job,
Whistling as they washed their large hands in the dark.
What they didn't know was that the goat's head was already
Singing behind them in the tree. What they didn't know
Was that the goat's head would go on singing, just for them,
Long after the ropes were down, and that they would learn to listen,
Pail after pail, stroke after patient stroke. They would
Wake in the night thinking they heard the wind in the trees
Or a night bird, but their hearts beating harder. There
Would be a whistle, a hum, a high murmur, and, at last, a song,
The low song a lost boy sings remembering his mother's call.
Not a cruel song, no, no, not cruel at all. This song
Is sweet. It is sweet. The heart dies of this sweetness.

ROISIN KELLY

TAIWAN

You were the Buddha I bowed to on the cold
stone floor of my life. That was paradise.
My forehead pressed to your statue's feet, I honoured
your temple's silence as you stared
at the shadows above me. Praying with incense
and oil, I still longed for the fruit
of the doorway's sunlit promise: white beaches
and whispering forest. Day and night I listened
to the ocean's caverns where water poured through water
below a sliced green surface.
                        But my feet
never knew the cold shock of the South China Sea.
My wrists were never blessed by pink blossoms.
You never kissed me below that wild foreign sun.
I left by a different doorway, a damp passage
that led towards darkness, felt my way by carvings
cut deep into the stone. There is old, and there is old
like the gorse-scorched hills of home
where I emerged barefoot, alone and crowned
with a twist of the hawthorn's white flowers.

LUKE KENNARD

ALL OF WHICH WAS MAYBE TOO MUCH TO GO INTO ON OUR FIRST SOCIAL ENGAGEMENT, BUT I FELT LIKE WE HAD AN AFFINITY

You're as bad as the last Unitarian I dated. I'm trying
to tell you how the water feels: A network of cities in the brain.

But you think the wide-mouthed vat of miracles pours as copious
on the prefab shack of school chairs / the cathedral 800 died raising.

At the wishing-well's margin you wish for disappointment, I wish
that the opposite of coffee existed and then I think in the 18th century

we would meet in a gravel pit to discuss the Psalms because that was
        the least
consecrated place we could think of: a gravel pit! The ever-changing,
        shingly surface;

our thin soles; hum of rudimentary machines, fine sand in our nostrils
coagulating into a toxic paste, occasional stab of flint or an elbow...

Because a King is a tyrant or a keyring novelty,
because a Lord is a landowner with a lifetime peerage,

What should we rename our God? The sound a PC makes
when you switch it off? Three things: I'm sorry for your loss;

Your scarf is pretty; I'd like to take you somewhere far away
where the air is more delightfully opaque. I know

I am the heart's estate agent. I know the cuffs of my trousers
trail unholy water wherever we go. I know. I know. I know.

VICTORIA KENNEFICK

THE LIFE YOU SAVE MIGHT BE YOUR OWN

The air-conditioned auditorium of a university campus,
cicadas sweat through high windows behind us.
Flannery O'Connor sneaks up the stairs
to take her seat in the dark, and to stare.

She shuffles down in her chair
(she'd die if we knew she was there),
already dead and so amused by the catch.
Showtime, the blue door swings open on its latch.

From its hatch they creep, breaking into a millipede canter
across the cool linoleum floor that squeaks with their banter.
The Annual Flannery O'Connor Conference, the O'Connference.
Purgatory's a scream, such a confluence.

Professor Pine pounds his fist on the podium like a preacher,
words whistle from his horseshoe teeth, trot up to reach her.
Flannery's a priest in a dress, no interest in kissing,
(in the gods she thinks of what she's been missing).

Professor Avery is soft as snow, she doesn't buy it.
Flannery had lips, hips, heat in there, don't deny it,
and (even) a womb, (Flannery blushes when she thinks
of that tomb). Of her pale-eyed Bible salesman. The cup.

Now no one will shut up,
the man with a limp, the girl with a squint,
they chatter, they argue, they gesticulate wildly.
Apostates, true-believers, she eyes them up slyly.

She pulls a pistol from her silk stockings.
Her eyes are dark and her smile is mocking.
She shoots them one after the other, out go the lights.
Grandmothers pray to God, academics cry for their wives.

A pile of bodies stacked high in the room,
not the point, don't look, it will be over soon.
The blood of the Saviour drips over each face,
the sense of an ending, the action of grace.

MIMI KHALVATI

PRAYER

for Hafez

Between the living and the dead,
May your memory be green.
In the book beside my bed,
May your signature be seen.

May your memory be green
For every lover, every spring.
May your signature be seen
Inscribed on every living thing.

For every lover, every spring,
Breathing clouds against the frost
Inscribed on every living thing,
Sees how every breath is lost;

Breathing clouds against the frost,
Because breath is always warm,
Sees how every breath is lost
In the one beloved form.

Because breath is always warm,
Hafez, when a lover gives his word,
In the one beloved form,
It is your voice that is heard.

Hafez, when a lover gives his word
In the book beside my bed,
It is your voice that is heard
Between the living and the dead.

JANET R. KIRCHHEIMER

BLESSING

I long for stones to put under my head,
to dream of a ladder that reaches
into the sky, where angels go up and down,
to know that God was in this place,

to take stones, and set them as a pillar, pour oil
on the top, wait to give name to
that place, wait for someone to call out
what they have found so I will know what I have lost.

I long, too, for fluidity, for rain to release me
from my vows, to give thanks for every drop,
to fill my mouth with song as the sea is with water,
and my tongue with praise as the roaring waves,
to be incandescent, iridescent, volatile.

CALEB KLACES

A NOTHING TO DO WITH GOD

1996, at the bus stop, my friend, mouth brown with Marmite
        and the paler brown of nicotine,
dressed up for the last, non-uniform, day of term
        in a Kappa tracksuit brought back from Zante,
electric blue with silver trim, asked hadn't my dad once
        been a pope or something?

I liked the idea of the Sistine Chapel, that it had been larger
        than Michelangelo's life. Larger than
a football pitch. Too large to take in? I asked my father,
        wanting him to nod his head solemnly.
It's still a general rule, that things should be larger
        than they are here, him older then

than he is now. And what an idea
        that a day could be ruined. The morning was still
as it had been before I kicked my sister
        under the train table coming home
from the old bombed Coventry Cathedral. In the new one

there is a photograph of two charred beams
        that fell in such a way as to resemble a crucifix.
And there is the crucifix hung on the wall
        like one charred beam fallen on another.

My father said nothing to do with God
        but looked intently towards nothing in particular
above the altar as he gave us coins
        to drop in the model of the cathedral
inside the cathedral.

Not yet thirty and already a star, Andreas Vesalius
      renounced the study of anatomy.
No longer should I willingly spend long hours
      in the Cemetery of the Innocents
turning over bones, nor go to Montfaucon to look at bones.
      Nor should I care to be locked out of Louvain
so that I might take away bones from the gibbet.

      But he could not entirely stop
and never failed to visit any nearby medical school,
      nor to inspect the bodies on the battlefield.

★

My father hitch-hiked to Israel in 1960
      and took notes. As the train pulled out
of the station, he realised that his bag was gone.
      Would he still have become a priest,
and then not one, he asks me, if he had returned
      from Israel and Naples and Belgrade
with his notebooks – if he had
      had, after repatriation from Rotterdam
by boat, his own account of himself?

★

      Bound for Venice, after his trip
to the Holy Land, the reasons for which are lost,
      in 1564, a storm took apart his boat
and with its remains Vesalius was washed up on Zakynthos,
      the island on which the tar was dredged
that failed to protect the ship, and which is known now
      by British tourists as Zante.

Where precisely he landed is not known, nor do we know
  where he was buried, by whom.
There seems little doubt, at least,
    that this was in the month of October.

ANJA KONIG

OCTOBER

The world being
praiseworthy
I went
and in the early morning
bought a pen.

YAHIA LABABIDI

BREATH

Beneath the intricate network of noise
there's a still more persistent tapestry
woven of whispers, murmurs and chants.

It's the heaving breath of the very earth
carrying along the prayer of all things:
trees, ants, stones, creeks and mountains alike.

All giving silent thanks and remembrance
each moment, as a tug on a rosary bead
while we hurry past, heedless of the mysteries.

And, yet, every secret *wants* to be told
every shy creature to approach and trust us
if only we patiently listen, with all our senses.

ANDREW LANSDOWN

PRAYER

Oh, for my mother in her pain,
Almighty and all-loving Lord,
I come to plead with you again.

For years her body's been a bane
That's put all gladness to the sword:
Oh, for my mother in her pain!

Too much misery makes a stain
To black all light and block all laud:
I come to plead with you again.

Today at least relieve the strain
And give reprieve as a reward,
Oh, for my mother in her pain.

I know there is no other Name.
Despite the fact my faith is flawed,
I come to plead with you again.

Although my many sins maintain
That I deserve to be ignored —
Oh, for my mother in her pain
I come to plead with you again!

SHARON LARKIN

BOND

You're going to have to explain.
I cannot understand
why you press this money into my hand
then close my fingers over it.

I do not know if it is mine to keep,
to take out later, look at, turn over,
remember.

I know I cannot simply toss
it into purse or pocket
with common coin.

I cannot tell if it is payment, reward,
deposit, float, capital, gift,
or all of these;
whether to donate it to a good cause
lock it in a vault,
buy seed, grow crops, harvest,
sell and buy more.

It is gold, I see that —
a rare thing, from a treasury.
It's slump-proof.

Night and morning, when my eyes are closed,
you place it into my palm again,
apply gentle pressure,
curl my fingers to cover it.

I fear I must use it soon
or you'll take it back,
give it to someone who understands.

But the greater fear is that I use it,
you give me more,
expect more in return.

SARAH LAW

WOMAN OF ROME

Meditation on moments from the Book of Margery Kempe

Here I am, not belonging
to anyone at all, except,
perhaps, a Divinity who listens
like a baby in the womb,
a lover to beloved –
I'm calling in the song's words:
Who am I to speak of mystery:
she raises the stone cup and says
drink me. All the birds fly up,
merriness is heaven-on-the-wing.

Drink me. All the birds fly up:
she raises the stone cup. And says
Who am I to speak of mystery.
I'm calling in the song's words:
lover, to beloved,
like a baby in the womb,
perhaps. A Divinity who listens
to anyone at all. Except
here I am. Not belonging.
Still the birds fly home.

SYDNEY LEA

THE PASTOR

I have just one person left on earth who's been
My friend through grade school, high school, church, and sports,
The pastor says. Meanwhile the winter rain
Explodes on the metal roof like handgun shots,

And it's hard to hear the man go on: *Thing is,*
He's lost his memory. There comes a catch
In his throat, something that none of us has witnessed
Through all the pastor's ministry. *Here's the trouble,* he adds,

I'm left alone with the things we knew together.
Silence ensues, save for a few quiet coughs,
And rustlings of the worship programs' paper.
Then the preacher seems to change his theme right off,

Speaking of Mary, and how she must have suffered
When her son referred to his apostolic peers
As family, not to her or to His brothers,
Not to Joseph — as if He forgot the years

Spent in their household, as if He kept no thought
Of ties that bind. The congregants are old.
They try to listen, but their minds go wandering off
To things like the pounding rain outside, which is cold

And ugly and loud. The storm, so out of season,
So wintry, still improbably recalls
The milder months, which vanished in a moment,
And which they summon vaguely, if at all.

JASON LEE

SETI

No longer sold on the wisdom of priests,
philosophers or televangelists,
now we've taken it upon ourselves
to eavesdrop on God, the heavens themselves.

We refuse to give up the ghost. At first
we listened, microwaving the skies,
then looked, crowding our collective eyes
to scan the planosphere, its pixelated art.

A Rorschach in extremis, we peer intently,
forcing ourselves to make sense of it all,
that great boxed hope we've come to expect,
absolving our follies, our petty feuds.

And perhaps, not wanting to seem too keen,
we project our best selves forward,
no mention of wars or devastation,
only a strained 'goodwill from planet Earth'.

Waiting. We have been waiting too long,
with our lenses too wide, our senses euphoric.
Our ten million signs shrink to a thousand,
to none, regressing infinitely,

so all that remains is to look imploringly
at the sky, those nebulous clouds,
across that unbearable emptiness,
to know finally, we are all alone.

JOHN B. LEE

UNCLE RUSS AND THE LITTLE HORSE

after the picnic
Uncle Russ
spoke freely
of riding his wise horse
the one
who loved to round up
the cattle, the one
whose ears
perked at the gate
and would not
surrender the strays
even in winter
when the pasture
was a cold far country
and wind
was white and damp with sleet
I could see
as he told us
that the pony he rode
was alive
in the telling
and the wind in his grin was
a wind he believed in
where the night and the snow
shook their mane
and this is my God
the God of natural wonder
the God of these
come-to-life horses
the past in my heart

like a wave
that carries
the light to the shore

MARY LEE

CELTIC CIRCLE

The Cross stands steadfast,
silent before the winds
of an open firmament; stately
in its weather-beaten stance,
storms blow through its eyes
that refuse to spill secrets.

When horizontal and vertical selves
coalesce within the cross's circle:
passion fires daily duties, elevates
worries, grounds yearnings.

I lean on this sacred tree, invite
it to root and shelter me, let
surrender shake routine, free
me to travel wholeheartedly.

WES LEE

IF IT COULD BE SERVED

All that unconscious loaf of childhood
I would eat again if it could be served.
If it could be served I would cycle the track by the river
to pick banana passionfruit hanging in cascades
from the tallest trees; yellow skin unzipped,
their seeds like the never-ending
pips of the pomegranate we would prick
with a pin at Christmas.
If it could be served I would have a friend
who asked no questions and raced
to climb a tree, fell and bashed their knee then laughed
through the snot and the wiped away tears
like a smear of life.
If it could be served I would be one
of two, and sometimes a gang,
with spears crafted from bulrush
and *toi toi*, charged over sand dunes
that waited for our first morning prints.

MELISSA LEE-HOUGHTON

ROWS AND ROWS OF TERRACED HOUSES, STRANGERS MOUTHING MY NAME

Sixteen. True summer dead like virtue, winter coming on deep –
the mornings were senile, sick yellow and bitter as pills, geraniums,
     blood –
I prayed as I slipped and stuttered on black ice
on the ring-road, going to market with its bastards and crooks,
     all of them
ready to snatch the love out of my teenage heart, out of my hand –
I prayed because I was bruised inside,
in a place so small only a prayer would fit and you couldn't
see or feel it, not when he brought me a cup of tea and I
avoided eye contact, not when he cracked.
The mornings were senile because he didn't remember
that he dragged me across the floor with my legs splayed.
I was a girl. I prayed to the future, the sun, birds, eyes, scars;
I prayed to loneliness, emptiness, ovaries –
I prayed for a kind of peace, that never set eyes on me.
Whoever I prayed to, they had their eyes closed, they were ashamed
and embarrassed by the
swollen parts and the beating and beating
and banging and banging and with my head over the toilet –
sick yellow and bitter as pills and geraniums and blood.
I nearly swallowed back my prayers and let them infect my body
in silence. In silence I decided it was the dead that listened, that heard –
but then I found my courage,
and I still prayed to you, regardless, my lord.

DOROTHY LEHANE

MIRROR

Call this paean or addenda;
a tiny buffered appendix,
a scarlet ibis. Call this
mimicry of the vastness,
think chime and parallel,
unstable universe, sturdy minds,
lexical ladders, dyslexic cadence.
We are nothing if not fluxed,
sweltering inside our fervent atlas,
violence is stability, nothing
if not resilient, tiny villains,
bullfighters obliterating,
clashing melting pots, metropolis
road rage, political hurricanes.
Else we are blanched out,
silenced, melancholic,
nothing happening for aeons,
familial fractures, splinter groups,
calm little quotas, glottal paused,
auspicious in silence, philosophers
on the fringes.

PHILLIS LEVIN

LENTEN SONG

That the dead are real to us
Cannot be denied,
That the living are more real

When they are dead
Terrifies, that the dead can rise
As the living do is possible

Is possible to surmise,
But all the stars cannot come near
All we meet in an eye.

Flee from me, fear, as soot
Flies in a breeze, do not burn
Or settle in my sight,

I've tasted you long enough,
Let me savor
Something otherwise.

Who wakes beside me now
Suits my soul, so I turn to words
Only to say he changes

Into his robe, rustles a page,
He raises the lid of the piano
To release what's born in its cage.

If words come back
To say they compromise
Or swear again they have died,

There's no news in that, I reply,
But a music without notes
These notes comprise, still

As spring beneath us lies,
Already something otherwise.

JACK LITTLE

ADHAN IN DAR ES SALAAM

Rich and full like tree sap, the call to prayer tipped hot wax
upon my back. I tingled on the sticky streets of Dar es Salaam,

imagined strong men with rippling voices, watched the infinite fall
       of a rock
into a lake, took pleasure in how the sound only lasts for a moment...

I devoured it, craved it – an addiction. Yet, on returning home,
my desire waned as my *Adhan* lost its truth. *Eid* passed false
with cold winds biting at the window panes, the sun folded
       behind the moon.

I cling to faith, hang it heavy around my neck,
hold a thousand guilty doubts:

My soul was scorched in Dar es Salaam
for the call to prayer began a hopeless search,
a song of truth I will never understand, and if I did,

could never truly embrace.

PIPPA LITTLE

HOLDFAST

You are the farthest north of your life.
He breaks a lichen stem from its silver birch,
Lays it in your hand. You have the urge
To fling it down, let its soft white
Bleached-out corsage slip away
But something halts you: turning it over
Now you see dung-brown velvet of cast-off antler –
All's slant here, you think, the way
You can only see some stars by squinting –
Then remember that city tree, grown
Through the metal frame of its sapling home
So wire curls burst from the bark in shark-tooth glinting:
What began as cradle turned to cage.
Its attachment shapes us most, he says.

MIKE LOVEDAY

SANCTUS

... he asks of the angel: why are our wings so badly bruised, if they belong to God?

... he asks of God: why, if we curl up and listen within, do we discover the muse sharp as a swallowed needle hiding in our belly?

... he asks of the muse: will she answer with more than an echo, this other who hears his ravings?

... he asks of the other: how do the angels balance us, between the body without pain, and the mind without calculation?

HELEN LOVELOCK-BURKE

PART OF DAY

This
the part of day
that is practice
for death.

It has power only to rest
as light rests
when duty ties it down
to wait for night.

In this hour words
from forgotten prayer
echo the unrecorded shapes
that formed in the silences
of childhood.

ROB A. MACKENZIE

AFTER EPIPHANY

The temporary lights are dead
spots, routine illumination,
blunting surprise, it seems,
incessantly. Cars pass through
like the elephants God drives
through eyes blank as needles.
We feel sorry for the camels,
down in the humps, grinning.

Their applause falls flat as rain.
What was impossible now feels
possible and passably mundane.
The Magi brood before the stars
fade to ordinary time, to dawn
camels, to elephants of God.

JEFFREY MACKIE

SIDEWALK MESSIAHS

They say that 'cleanliness is next to godliness'
And I am a mess.
I
Want saintliness.
I want to be reckoned with
Given a purpose, a name
A reason
To be happy with myself.
Read books, still looking for
A character, a faith
I can put my image on
Hang myself upon
Prop myself up upon.

I walk down St. Catherine
On an Autumn afternoon
Take every pamphlet from every pamphleteer
Between Stanley and McGill College
I join and discard a few religions
But I keep the pamphlets.
And they keep returning, back when they promised
Autumn afternoon messiahs
And they keep coming
Is it in my eyes?
Do they see into my heart?
Do they know how many hearts I've broken?
How many times I have broken my own?

'Jews for Jesus' have the best T-shirts
Hare Krishna I can't get into
Their uber-joy seems a bit cynical

But they have the cutest women
Even with their shaved heads
Aaaah! give them six months
Celibacy is hell when you're cute
And the boy believer beside you
Is so intense –
Maybe they'll take off, plant some trees
The world will be a better place
Because two people want it to be.
In the meantime I will finish
The Last Temptation of Christ.

In the meantime:
I will go back to my working day
I am on Rue St. Catherine
Where even the stoplights promise sex
Where every corner promises, a crossing
Where I get joy and anger
And I want to join the men
Wearing the old school sandwich boards
Promising doom.
Feels like Times Square 1946
And once again I realize
I don't know what I want
I want to dance to Franz Ferdinand
I want to go to a monastery
I want to read every book I already own.

Winter sky 3 A.M.,
Reading Free Will Astrology
We all want to know how tomorrow will be
Burning popcorn, choking on the smoke
With no cable, the TV is off
Too tired to surf
I know joy, but sadness
Knows how to find my heart

Corrall my thoughts
I have faith, though not as certain
As the St. Catherine Messiahs.

DZEKASHU MACVIBAN

WAYS OF SEEING

We've found salvation in different places —
In the awareness of the saviour
With tramps in cheap motels on forlorn highways
In our first million
In a bacchanalian orgy
In the pages of a book
In the process of immolation
In lonely prison cells
And O, in the arms of the muse.

MARY MADEC

THE NIGHT I MET JESUS ON A DUBLIN BIKE

Who is that man cycling on ahead
who looks back to check I'm keeping up
a little amused perhaps by my struggle
through the traffic.
All I know is that he has a heart —
the conclusion of little details —
how he remembers what I say
and holds my words like a shaman.
This is what I think as I spin
through the air from Blessington basin
and down by Belvedere,
where we stop.
He bends down to put on
my visibility anklet
joking that now I'll be able to put
my best foot forward
as we go with the wind down the quays.
I'm too focused to notice
the distractions of the city
on the side.
At the lights he goes on ahead
his visibility vest dazzling
and the light of his helmet
flickering like a sanctuary lamp.
Our destination, a pizzeria
where we sit and eat,
chat about where we've been
where we'll go from here.

MAITREYABANDHU

STAR MAN

He saw a blue light entering his heart
coming from a man he couldn't see
but knew was standing in the stars above
the playing field behind the house. The light
came like the curl of candle smoke and lit
a cooking-apple tree inside his head
where he'd built a den and brought flowers
in a broken mug without its handle.
He could see the usual things – the laurel hedge,
the path that marked the border of his world –
but no river murmured powerful thoughts,
no wind of meaning blew among the stars,
no nature's heart beat full against his own,
just apple branches lit up in the dark.

ALICE MAJOR

THE GOD OF SPARROWS

observes
the multifarious detail,
the minutiae of feather, fact,
flight, flick, fleck, egg,
mite
is
a bright round eye.

CHRIS MANN

A SMALL CHURCH IN THE DRAKENSBERG

If you're out driving through the foothills of the Drakensberg
don't miss the signs that edge your road in sun and rain.
One leads to what looks like a shed made out of planks of wood
whose knots and cracks are weathered in the grain.

One calm bright day in spring I parked my car beside its fence
and sat a while to take in what was there.
It was I think as you'd expect – a rusted gate, a tangled path,
a dove that flew up into a forest's sun-streamed air.

The small arched windows in the sides were boarded up,
the graves were lost in grass below dark cypress trees,
but brooding on the path I shut my eyes and prayed a while,
and praying heard the steadfast hum of bees.

It was as if they lived within a country in full bloom.
Beside the porch, a pew stood in the knee-high grass,
among warped fascia boards, old hymn-books in a box,
discarded chairs and shards of dusty window glass.

The porch door was ajar. I peered into a gloom and glimpsed
stacked pews, half-sanded walls and altar rails,
an altar like a workbench where a carpenter had left his tools,
wrapped panes of glass, new sanding discs and nails.

The scent of sanded yellowwood hung in the hot still air.
It shaped my wintered faith's fresh wakening.
The dark gold gathered light inside that small dim church
was Christ stored in a honeycomb of spring.

KIRYA MARCHAND

APARTMENT 16

Me?
I am nothing
like God

the breath in the marshes
that bothers the curtains.

You are trying to read
you think, God is trying to reach me
I once caught him creeping

through the office window,
where the bugs got in.

God remember how we treated them?
How we repented when the infestation began

with caulked screams
the susurrus of insects
us, listening, as it swallowed our bed
in its pestilence.

My books were the last to be eaten.
Everything left hidden in the margins became

nothing
like God

the breeze through the streets, how
sorry it seems.

KATHRYN MARIS

STREET SWEEPER

God scatters where he eats.
The sweeper wheels his cart to what falls.

The broom assembles a pile.
The wind dismantles the pile.

God is the messy wind. The pile
is the mouthpiece of the wind.

Sometimes the wind is bluster.
Sometimes the wind is a mute.

There is the God who listens.
There is the God who speaks.

The God who listens is a gentle liar.
The God who speaks is laconic and hard.

I ask if I'm loved.
He points to the graveyard his garden abuts.

I clutch his hair. I say *Am I loved?*
He claims his love for me is deep

but zealless. Over the garden wall,
the God who listens, the neighbour,

smiles when I ask if I am loved.
He points to the God across the wall,

the first God, the God I just left,
as if to say *God loves you*.

Sometimes he speaks through his dog.
Sometimes he doesn't speak.

If his mother tongue were 'dog'
or 'frog' or 'wind' or 'rubbish'

could I learn that language
and hear that I was loved?

Or would the answer
be something I couldn't hear.

The Periodic Table won't revoke
what it has put in the world –

Earth metals, non-metals, catalysts.
It is God's slovenly generosity

and is difficult to gather,
as the street sweeper knows,

as the wind knows, as I know, and God knows.
The sweeper smiles at me lovingly

like the silent god,
the one with the message I cannot hear.

JAKE MARMER

LOOPHOLE

Rabbi Ashi said: [On Sabbath], when lying on a straw bed, you must not move a straw with your hand, yet you may move it with your body. – Babylonian Talmud, Sabbath 50A

If you must move
that which can't be touched
move it,
touching it
in a way no one would ever think of touching it.
Being something that doesn't happen
it won't happen.
There won't be a word to describe what you're doing –
you can get as close as you like.
And this is the secret of closeness:
to the centre
of great untouchable
   moving
towards you like a gullible bird
moving straight
into your Talmudic glove,
set at the gaping mouth
of the loophole.

ALWYN MARRIAGE

ELEMENTAL

Water first,
burst of creativity
born of chaos
swirling in impenetrable dark

impossible to contemplate
that anyone could pass through sea
as dry as bone, then turn to witness
an enemy's destruction in the water

led by a man,
like Adam made from dust
(as opposed to Eve
who came from human stock),

who later learned,
in special circumstances,
to strike a rock,
and let the water flow

but didn't realise
that water never could extinguish
the fire that burns deep in the centre of it all
or even, on occasion, keeps a bunch of briars alight.

BARBARA MARSH

THINGS MY MOTHER LEFT UNSAID

Once, when you were trying to finish
your embroidery, a gift to me, in your hospital bed,
I asked was there anything you wanted
to talk about; not just then, you said,
you were too tired. You never told me what you thought
about dying. I didn't press you. I knew
you believed God knew what He was doing,
that darkness was not what you would face
but the open arms of your grandmother and Aunt
Marguerite – whose eyes I have, you said,
who died when you were a child – this was your
unshakeable fact. If I pray, it is for your belief,
that you were spared the nothing I face: the daily
scramble on a dry hill, the earth-bound slide.

TOBY MARTINEZ DE LAS RIVAS

SHIGGAION

the bare naked field is thy part, as
   the cat all eyes and bemes and flame
couches into the shell of that vexed
   gorgeous chest, she is a rose, is a for-

knowing beyond *thee*, colossal in
   thy ignorance, thy field blight, as *thy*
black stinking potatoes, *thy* milt,
   alii dicebant haec verba non sunt da-

monium habentis numquid daemo-
   nium potest caecorum oculus aperire.
So. Tarmac wildfire on the protest
   road where nothing in chains, like a-

nother day rising, a man teetering
   on the edge of a desk on tiptoes, feet
scrabbling, his neck is in a noose,
   such is *thy* part, *crownede wyth reytes*

bere mee to thy leathall tyde, bear
   me, if you can and if the back straight
as a buttercup stalk permits you, if
   it is allowed & approved by communal

delete all reference to such, sinful,
   man is alone, so scuttle back & forth
across my patriotic Brunel Clifton
   bridge of a riveted back, the rest sold,

here is the sink of my, my stinking
    vulgate body, dicebant autem multi ex
ipsis daemonium habet et insanit
    quid eum auditus, it is the dogma, it is

the capital has done this to my so
    shining brow, Blodewydd, rendering
the glue from the butchered bone
    boiling down the surplus immaterial

capital of a nation: you want, you
    buy it, why should I say one direct
thing, why? Does the goshawk, its
    wingtip pivoting around the inward

arc of its turning circle as the finch
    breaks cover from beneath the tarred
bird table, authentic rural design,
    the serried fir trees as dead in the land

as their tenders care a shite for the
    for the proper grammar? It *is* grammar,
the purity of design, the framework
    shaking, never collapsing until finally

permitted to do so. So you stitch
    your hair, my graceful fled love, and so
everything is the winterlong light
    of certain flowers and birds I can't name

and am proud to do so. The bridge
    is depravity, the road, the government,
the centre of fear and betrayal, just
    act within your proscribed bounds, as

the goshawk and the leaping joyful
   cat refuse to do, beak & teeth in the crop
and the bright blood, foamy as alco-
   hol, the darling berries in October again:

that is how it all was and will never
   never be, facta sunt autem encenia in Hiero
solymis et hiemps erat. The going
   down of that eyelid, and it was winter.

NANCY MATTSON

DEAD END

She left only fifteen letters
unearthed from a cellar
no gravestone no record of death
no fate   no what-else
no more plans but I stand on this plot
among half-bare trees
shoulder to shoulder with three
who know her name
and the need for certainty blood
disappears

into the moment we plant
on Eino and Tamara's grave
cloth flowers
whose colours would make me sneer
anywhere else but here in Karelia

I declare lilies
orange for Saskatchewan
pronounce roses
pink for Alberta
white for Finland
red for Russia
their fluorescence
so bizarre it embarrasses
borders into dissolving

the long search ends *our father* tumbles unbidden
out of the mouth *hallowed be thy* brokenness
releases tears *on earth as it is* cuts to the heart
of words gone old and dull   splits them open

to the core of prayer   scraping the throat
one by one as never before

a hard swallow a way to breathe
a voice takes words by the tongue
through   *trespass against*
and *thine is the kingdom*

wood never dies   *amen*

NYLA MATUK

BEGGING THE QUESTION

The question had doubled.
        It's amplification we're after, after all.

The mirror reflected him.
He knew some other civilization
was looking down on him from the long
enjoyment of its enlightenment.

A beam is a beam and a path.

        The path to certainty is
        customarily taken alone.

The terminus had a stake in it.
Leviathan ironwork of a Victorian footbridge
was a price to pay.

        The lamp pointed at him and laughed!
        So the mirror showed him up, too,
        preening like a circus,
        waiting for him to see the light.

BEN MAZER

GETHSEMANE

You were insane, and I was sane,
now you are sane, and I'm insane.
I met you first in Gethsemane
when you are gone, and I remain.
The gardens there were lightly flush
at introduction of your blush
the kissing shadows nightly touch
time shadows render from the flesh.
The very bushes seemed to move
with attitudes approaching love
at the last moment to reprove
as if they didn't want enough.
Where earlier entering the town
calm was embedded in renown
(directly it descends from this
perfect betrayal of a kiss).
The stirring petal on the bush
ignited by the kiss of flesh
the fragrance stirring in the air
shimmering like a distant star
the evidence that you are there
though even now it seems so far.
When you are gone, we meet again
when like a shadow fame and name
are predictably the same.
Men view the son, the desert plain;
when you are gone, we meet again.

ERICA McALPINE

PROOF

after Horace Odes 1.34

Having been but a slight and infrequent
worshipper of the gods, and having roamed awhile,
expert in mistaken wisdom, today
I've been forced to set sail —

to renew a course I'd forsaken. You see,
Jupiter, who needs the clouds to throw
his lights, has driven, just now,
his clattering horses and chariot

through a clear blue sky,
so that the ground and the sea,
the river Styx's source and I
all were forcibly shaken. That's power —

enough to make high things low and low things
high, to humble the strong and lift the obscure.
From one man Fortune steals the crown;
on another she delights to place it.

SUSAN McCASLIN

STEADY STATE

You follow Spirit up the ladder
or She follows you

Who's following whom?
you wonder, then land

on a rung of being
well past judgment

but not discernment
of the big landscape

to which you belong
with your thumping animal heart

with all its everyday amazements –
ant's trek, whale's bewildering song

Presto! As if this were enough
and so it is, as you finger

the wood's worn grain
imprints of bare feet

signs of others' playing
up and down the stair

for so it is, not ladder
but stair, spiralling

No thing above
no thing below —

only this intertwining
rest into action

this mystery
betwixt and between

MARION McCREADY

AUTUMN TREES

Autumn trees are effigies
burning in the streets.

They lose their leaves, their wings,
wind-driven

into every corner, crevice,
upturned hand.

These falling prayers,
these harvest psalms.

The bloodied skins of them
shirring the ground.

Harbingers. Little deaths,
they harp at my feet

words begging to be said,
words begging to be freed:

two men shall be in a field,
one shall be taken, the other one left.

COLIN McDONALD

DAYS LIKE THIS

Luca tries to edge the continental United States next to El Salvador,
and next to me, in the throes of a speech impediment,
Elliot is waiting for a word or two that starts with m
to come to him. I wait for days like this,

before the traffic of snow-shoveled boots and medical
immunization forms; the mothers who I'm friends with
and the fathers I could be by now, and when

it's just the three of us, or four, I could call
days like this my doubt, as if I chose
impermanence; my plastic cup – the habiliments
of tea – arranged like a wet rag against my lips, as if to demonstrate

my injury; my countenance hand-painted, hung with string
like phytoplankton. 'Is it true
that bombs are buried

underground?' asks Elliot, feet touching the floor
he can't, hand tracing the sound
as if by memory. I watch the letter m persist
like koi on sandpaper, the dawn's light a reminder

to look down. Like God, I am mistaken
for a setting, am presumed to belong
in one place – a shaker of salt

and testosterone – the skin of table polish raised
like mountains on a map beneath
my elbows, rendered glossy, smeared,
like pages in a magazine, interred in glare. 'In places

far away, it's true,' I say, as the U.S. begins to blur
the ocean's pale, scored surface,
channeling its absence like a syllable,

a starting place. 'M-m-m,' I say,
as if to replicate the recent past, to speak my mind in gestures
I can't obfuscate. Our presence here
is obvious, I think, where words should be –

one man's, sung as if swallowed once
to catch himself, who can't decide
if to teach is, temporarily, to watch – and read

a poem from the beginning, as if to accommodate
my preferences. 'I'm Nobody,' I tell them. 'Are you
Nobody – too?' But Elliot keeps answering
the questions of the poem. 'I'm Elliot,' he says, and laughs,

'Are you?' but that's the end
of that. *It isn't difficult to entertain a child,*
I admit, humiliated, in the margins

of Emily Dickinson. In group lesson, I focus on
the concept of time passing; the word for after
winter, after spring. After Newtown,
which Google no longer equates

to a massacre, I couldn't remember
the code to enter the building. That morning,
I stood shivering, failing to recite

the 4, the 3, the 8, the 6, trying to become
a man with what I had: my distance, which became itself
a why and how. I'm 30 now, but like them,
indefatigable, unable to answer
my own questions. 'Can a man

be love for another man?' Elliot asks. I used to pay attention
to what I couldn't understand. I thought

that if I listened I would see myself
in every word I could resist, supplanting
its background like a beautiful sky's cloud. But here I am,
less apparent than a figure in a painting of a landscape,

keeping to himself a peace he cannot claim. 'Both of those words
start with m,' I say. 'And yes.' 'But-but-but
how do both men die?' But what he means is not together,

what's it like. You wonder if it's your responsibility
to turn death into metaphor, to speak of silence
or be quiet. When I talk about poetry,
I talk about our faculties for sight and sound

and touch, and how what we experience
probably happened. Sometimes we feel the carpet,
and then we go to the park. Luca is, all the time,

using the playground equipment the wrong way:
standing on the tunnel, going up the slide,
as if our days are numbered. Only if other adults are around
do I tell him it isn't safe.

RYK McINTYRE

METAPHORS ABOUT STARFISH JESUS

are like juggling seaweed: you can
try. Of course, you will end up looking
stupid. Don't say I didn't warn you.

Buddy, Starfish Jesus doesn't take
your shit. He didn't die and return just
to make the same mistakes again.

When he turns his cheek, believe it:
there will be a roundhouse kick
at the tail end of it. He didn't travel

to the Far East and fail to learn
a few things. This time, the tide
comes in with a can of Whoop-Ass

up front. Anyone caught idle, any
one with 'Footprints in the Sand'
on their lips gets the full benefit

of the Holy Dope-Slap. Times five.
His mistake was going with Meek
the first time. This round, it's War.

DORA E. McQUAID

ONE VOICE

Two days after I held my father as he died,
the priest comes to my parents' house to
meet with my mother, my two older brothers, and me
to plan my father's Funeral Mass.

In the living room, all of us perched in grief and tension,
my mother tells the priest she wants me to speak
in the church, during his Mass of Christian Burial.
The priest denies her, turning to me to tell me:
You are not a practicing Catholic.
You may not speak in the house of God.
We move on to choose psalms and prayers,
photos for the program.

Two days later, in the rain,
at my father's graveside, I speak then
for the first time. I do this one thing whose idea
has been the most horrifying thing my mind could imagine
for the entirety of my life.
Next to my father's coffin, above a hole in the ground
into which they will lower him when we all turn away,
I clear my voice.
I read the poem I wrote years ago, for my father,
about what and how he taught me to be
this woman that I am.
I do this horror because it is the response I had,
but did not offer, to the priest in my parent's living room,
that I have held within me to sustain me
through his viewing, his funeral mass, this moment.

You are not a practicing Catholic.
You may not speak in the house of God.

To this, I say:
I am the house of god.
We all are, each one of us.
And my speaking, using this voice
that God gave me, is memory of that.

I know this.

This is what my father taught me.

LEONA MEDLIN

NO STRAIGHT THING

So where's the point or points of trying?
Ruling a line to take that doesn't
cross the grain is easier thought than
drawn. Making a way that's both humane
and true is as likely as angels
in Peckham Rye. Still... we see what we
will. Imagine being it. The more
we make believe, the more we make it
so; turn, bend, twist and curl from point to
point – all awkward angles, but moving.

SIGHLE MEEHAN

WORLD WITH END

Sometimes dark is absolute. Dunlewy
where sleet falls sharp on Errigal and grey
winds wither the songlines of the gods,
where sunlight does not dare to cross
the Derryveagh and dimple
the shadow lands behind,
even here, in this dark place, even
when the moon shudders into hiding
and the night is starless, you can see
the sinews of the mountain
purple, muscled,
uneasy in submission.

Night driving through the midlands, remit
of Bridget, a female god, who ordained light,
decreed when night should wane
who chaperoned the moon, the stars
and now looks coldly on the pylon grid
tattooed onto her belly, graffiti
inked with tarmac on her vulva,
even here, in this dark place, even
when you stop the car and stand
in the pitch of nearly midnight, you can see
her contours
soft on the edge of blackness.

In your own bed, on a June evening
languorous in the swish of sea sounds
the soft spittle of a garden hose, a neighbour
mowing his lawn; time fractions.
Skewered on a pinprick of eternity,

you smell the sulphur, ash taste
in your mouth as viaticum
turns to dust. You see
the dark erupt, world without god,
the Alpha explained, the Omega
random,
absolute.

(Errigal is a mountain in the Derryveagh range in Dunlewy, Co Donegal, Ireland)

DANTE MICHEAUX

AUBADE ON A BLESSING

In the hush of morning,
at that time when autumn begins
to sharpen the wind to its will
and the golden hues of the earth are bright,
I watched the sun climb
the carillon of a church on the hill.
The light made visible a meager man
who stood on the eastern bank of the river,
whispering to a cherry tree,
in the sleep of its annual deadening –
and in the span of smallest measure did
pink blossoms split the gray-brown branches.
Black birds, from every direction, swooped
and landed at his feet, save one,
that alighted on his palm.
Favoring it among the others,
the man did feed this bird the tree's bursting fruit.

And the bird began to speak, cawing
this is the dawn that the comforter has come.

ALICE MILLER

BURN

Picasso sees a photo of Guernica at night
burning in a French newspaper.
A man says God is lost in
the novel, and when we put down
our books, spines-spread, we're left
with our own life's sentences
sweeping over our faces like waves
endlessly cresting
endlessly breaching
all over the sand, gold gone grey,
waves asking to wash out
what's said. Each word used on beaches,
on airstrips. It is difficult tonight
to tell air from skin. Difficult to find
your wordless controls
to gently land this plane
that is your only body.

CAMERON MILLER

MOTHER TERESA'S GOD

A response to the revelation that Mother Teresa reached out in vain for forty years
to be touched again by a God she encountered only once in personal revelation,
and even then only to send her into the streets of Kolkata.

I know you
who left that old woman out to dry
fried soul bacon crisp
from inside out

I know you
who left us stranded here
cynicism replacing grief
gangrenous Hundred Acre Wood

I know you
who shimmers on glassy water
never held never touched never heard
never known

I know you
who gags mystics with intimate fingers
swilling blood and tears
they starve swallowing

I know you
who snarls orders backstage
Oz-words on stone and papyrus
cocktails of bile and milk

I know you
who jilted the wrinkled nun and others
lunatic in crown of thorns
Baptist preacher shot in head

I know you
keep your distance
I will not be known
by you

I know you.

PATRICIA MONAGHAN

CELEBRATION OF THE ORDINARY

'Rule', it means: 'the order
of things'. From Latin ordo,
'a row or rank', from
an even older syllable
meaning 'to assemble
skillfully'. Ordinary:
sustaining tasks, how we
move through the day,
turning now and again in
comfortable familiarity, in
familiar comfort, to hold
each other's gaze. And
especially: the way of nature,
not just a garden's straight
rows but the winding paths
that deer cut on the prairie,
not only the season's patterns
but a week's changing weather.
'Ordinary' does not mean
predictable, unwavering,
routine, for there is order
seeded into chaos, whose
gorgeous twining patterns
are too huge to discern
from this garden on this day
when we plant ordinary
seeds in ordinary soil,
row upon row upon row,
while across the valley
deer skilfully assemble
networks of pathways
connecting the apple trees.

MILES DAVID MOORE

A MODERN NATIVITY

A noise at midnight in my garden shed
Drove the dog nuts. We stumbled out to see
A newborn baby sleeping peacefully
Inside a rag-stuffed wheelbarrow bed.
His mom and daddy stared at me with dread –
Two shabby working folks society
Cut loose. The single light bulb, hanging free,
Gathered a glow around the baby's head.

What happened next? I'm not sure I can say.
I can't describe just how I felt, or feel.
I heard a voice intoning, 'You can stay'.
It offered them some blankets and a meal.
The dog stopped barking, which is not his way.
I had no earthly clue a dog could kneel.

STEPHEN MORRISSEY

THE POSSIBILITIES OF APRIL: SECTION 7

The message is:
forgive everybody
no matter
what harm
they did
to us, there's
no recourse
in this life's
narrative,
the hurt
and anger,
throw it
overboard
from the sinking
ship of existence,
from the hold and
steerage, from the
watery decks
as waves crash
over this floor
of our defeat —

the spiral
circles grow
smaller,
a circular
decline
to the still
silent spot
of quietness
and completion,

that place
where we
awake to the
fragrance
of God's presence
which comes
uninvited
and momentary,
and then
is gone –

ANDREW MOTION

QUIVIRA

If only the stories had not been so delicious,
but from the day I first heard them I started
to embroider, and very soon was suggesting
a land far in the East where fish are as large
as horses, and even the minor administrators
eat off gold plates, and sleep on golden beds.
When the time came for us all to leave home
I have to admit I even believed them myself.
That is why I packed in my birchbark canoe
a robe made of feathers from more than 100
different kinds of bird that live in our forest.
So that when I had finally crossed the Ocean
I would have appropriate ceremonial dress
for my encounter with the Great Khan.

DAVID MUSGRAVE

THE DEAD
For my father

He has come back.
He has come from outside himself to assume
the proportions of dream, in a city of symbols falling
from deliverance, offered up to speech.
He mouths voiceless vowels, but cannot settle
in the complex room with unwashed windows
and sparse light in starfish and jellyfish shapes,
moving between moments. He is the sovereign
of helpless beauty, full of advice and all
dressed up with nowhere to go. Tears are not
required, there is not long, there is no need
for reassurance. Pigeons scrape the eaves.
He moves about restlessly, smiling
as if he had given himself over
to the sea or the lobes of harbour underlapping
the sky. Books are of no consequence,
he can no longer read. He understands
the weather and is interested in me.
Nights come by, from time to time, but mostly
days with a hard yellowness fix themselves
in his eye. He wears the clothes of a family
man and has no need for food. He needs
only a little time, enough for love.
He only wants to talk.

KARTHIKA NAÏR

MERIDIANS I

Half past three in Vellayani: they are waking
the gods, one by one, with conch shells that blow off warm
quilts of hush, rose-water baths and sandalwood scrubs
for sludge from the hesternal pleas of devotees
and a half-open lotus for each pair of feet
while day awaits in damp muslin by the temple
doorway, dripping light – and early, unformed blessings
that cupped paternal hands collect with the same hope
you must have held the parchment etching my future
thirty-five harvests back; then carry down a mile
of winding belief (morning rustling underfoot),
tiptoeing home to lay them along a headboard
whence they trickle on the snowdrift of a pillow,
and seep through folds of igneous, agnostic dreams.

MADELEINE NATTRASS

BROODY EMILY

Cooped up, coddling the unknown
knocking on that *Old Neighbour's* door
wanting to be friends with Him   yet infinitely wary
of the not-so-nice underside.

The way you questioned early – learned Rules
welcomed unknowing needed wonder.

The way you stretched your high mind around the
circumference
of the Divine taking a measure finding Its likeness
in earth's evanescent Things.

STEPHEN NELSON

NO-SELF DISCOVERY

I seem to have found it!

It is I. It is not I.

Let's call it Christ, because Christ is the constant in whom all
things manifest. It is Christ and I am. Yet I am not Christ. Such a
claim would be ridiculous. It is I.

You see the muddle I am in?

Ha! I have found it. Here it is. The I, the all in I. Christ. I have
it here in me like a bean. It appears transparent, flares up, moves
from my sight, then reappears, here, then here. I hold it in my
heart, cupped, in the palm of my heart, cupped, lovingly.

Christ the bean, which is I.

At sunset I almost had it, but it would have destroyed me. Red
sky spaciousness. It burned me, tore my eyeballs to shreds, left me
dumb and gaping. Such catastrophic beauty! The all in all in I.
Almost. It.

One place I find it is the bench up there. It comes happily
through the trees and the flies near the tyre factory, sits with me,
happily, as it should do, as it wants to. Jesus, I call it. Here it's a
gently exploding glass, a drenching in love. Here it sits. Jesus.

It leaps from the young lovers, to the family enjoying a summer stroll, to the little boy peddling his bicycle uphill. It leaps to me. It leaps like the moment you recognise the world and everyone in it, the I that they are. Yes, that's it! That's... oh everyone listen to the eye that's new in me not me. Swallow it whole! Digest it!

You as I.

You, not you.

Not I.

We seem to have found it. You in me, the I. It. Us.

MICHAEL NEWMAN

THE LORD'S SUPPER

There was no shining light,
No conversion outside Damascus.
I took up the elements as normal,
Watched the priest perform the blessing,
And then returned to my pew.
At what point prayer took over
I cannot answer.
There were no tongues of fire.
Yet later, at the Communion rail,
I felt risen in my putrefied flesh.
All that had been Void
Was filled with radiance:
Loving God, I could love others.

C.P. NIELD

PRAYER WHEEL

A circle forms a lotus in the brain,
Omnipotent and happy as the sun.
We turn the wheel and watch the world remain

An exiled god, whose broken words explain
Beyond the revolution of the gun.
A circle forms a lotus in the brain

To doubt that titan's rational disdain
And liberate the many from the one.
We turn the wheel and watch the world remain

A monkey full of wanderlust and pain.
May love describe a heart where there is none.
A circle forms a lotus in the brain,

A hunger to be lit in every vein –
To sit and face the ghost we cannot shun.
We turn the wheel and watch the world remain

A devil's revelation and refrain:
Our mind goes out the moment breath is done.
A circle forms a lotus in the brain;
We turn the wheel and watch the world remain.

KATE NOAKES

THE BARN SWALLOW'S CAROL

Families gather, but as you come to sing
by the child's crib, I'm far off on the wing,
so long gone south-due-south into the Berg
wind, not hidden, torpid, not cold-air hung.

I don't know of hoar frost, or snow on snow
on snow. Earth-iron, water-stone
are mysteries. Bleak ice makes no moan.

I'm swallow, what gifts can I bring? Fat gnats,
thick mud, new nests from fynbos or Cape Flats
mid-winter/mid-summer, all I can I share:
the dip-dive, the soar-swoop in fresh-fly-air.

DAN O'BRIEN

MY HANDWRITING

grew small for a time, Puritan
in the black ink I still favor. I felt compelled
to rein myself in, believing
the sin of pride governed me,
a child. I thought large print meant loud voice
and loud voice an affront
to God's ears. So I chastened myself to grow smaller
while still remaining
the great thing I was, still decipherable
to myself at least,
and if not to me then to God.

I had other sins, of course,
and prayers I knew by heart.

Or did I dwindle myself down
to this thread on the page
so my mother would find me
and ask, What's this?

NESSA O'MAHONY

MANTRA

Your brother came often those last weeks,
a limber version of you,
reminder of what might have been
had illness gone elsewhere.

He was convinced
the right arrangement of words
might see you through this,
a practice each night before sleep
to imprint subconscious belief
with recovery.

I daren't catch your eye,
the most articulate part
now the swallow was gone and the lips
refused to shape syllables in the right order.
An eye that could do fury, impatience, love
in quick succession.

But this time you nodded,
index finger graciously pointing
that visiting hours were up.

Seeing my uncle out,
I promised to do my best
to persuade the recusant,
remembering how your words
would help my passage into sleep.

Last thing each night,
you'd perch on the bed,
fold my hands in prayer
as I followed your lead:
Hello Holy God this is Nessa speaking,
God bless me and make me very good.
God bless my Mam and Dad,
and all my friends and relations, living and dead,
particularly my Granny in Cork,
and my Granny in Ballinasloe, and my Granddad.

The rhythm has stayed with me
40 years and more,
easing the wait in the dark,
forming my soul's belief
in the pattern of sounds.

I wasn't there when you passed,
can only guess if those words,
or any like them, were in your head;
did you greet your God,
ask your blessings for family and friends,
for the living, for the dead?

HELEN OVERELL

CANTICLE

And so there is inward sight
and what depth of colour
flows and fills
the heart

and this is different
from unwanted excess
caught on the snag
of a nail;
and within the silence
there is the thread of song,
as though a lark
on the wing

in some far reach of sky,
at one with light and life,
pours out her soul
and gathers

sound into beads of amber
and amethyst, jade and bone,
banded pebble,
rosewood.

JAN OWEN

WEST WINDOW

This woman with a baby on her lap,
upright as an iris stem
– one bloom, one bud –
holds in her poise all women
cradling the light of the world
in Syria, Sudan, Nineveh, Memphis, Ur.
Especially the one I sat with for an hour,
Thursday, the week of the bus strike,
in a rackety second-class train carriage,
the nine A.M. to town,
a plain woman smiling the wider
for a hare lip and the joy of
taking the baby on her lap,
Vietnamese, with a matching smile,
in for the surgery she herself never had.
A symmetry – that child, that woman,
nervous, elated, leaning a little
forward as she spoke, and beatific
in a sort of suburban way
being blessed for a moment with
the clarity of glass, a window, say,
through which I might have caught
a glimpse of the Nativity,
this window by which I now remember them.

WILLIAM OXLEY

AN ADDRESS

God, you have to be the ultimate good.
If not, you are not and nothing and nowhere.
Now, in the mid-point of this waste land
of miserable poems and lost loves –
that is: sorrow, self-pity and the broken
cycles of decent, dearest feelings,
I hear – yes, hear – a silence beyond
the sound of wind, bird chatter and
the greatest music mortals make –
the dynamic silence painters sometimes
capture, or scientists dub event horizon,
or philosophers the unmistakable contradiction
in human knowing, like conceiving
the ultimate good in a world where there is
no, yes, no ultimate good. God, sooner
or later you're going to have to show yourself:
a light that is? *Is* like feeling on fire.

RUTH PADEL

TO SPEAK OF DISTANCE

To speak of distance and the sanctuary lamp.
Something you have to do or find,
a world you must escape. Never mind
rumours of an immigration gate.
Revamp the passport. Speak of hope,

that cinnamon bird
born on the site of loss, with a thousand
resistance strategies frost-freckling her wings
like mica charms or ancient pilgrim songs
embossed in the Book of Psalms.

The task is to assimilate. To move
between the languages – in your case
Hebrew, Arabic, Aramaic, Greek –
and celebrate your journey to the shrine.
Everyone's crossing is a pilgrimage.

The hard thing is to pass; harder still
to fold those wings and drop the mask.
Just do it. Translate the old words
into new. You'll find fresh bearings
for a crossing-place. This is our exodus –

through cliffs of fall to a floating
island. Here is our constitution.
Here are the moon and sun
in never-before-seen positions
struggling to be heard.

MANDY PANNETT

SO SLIGHT

I am moved by the tale
of an anchorite
who sought the horizon's

opening place
the one quiet gap
where earth is not sealed to the sky.

There are pictures of him
stooping his shoulders, low as a mole
looking under and up –

What can he see?
A crystal sphere
with shutters that open
and close for the sun
a dangle and clatter of silver stars
bright in the welkin's blaze?
I would give him
a grey-green light
the shape of silence

and so slight an elevation
that sparrows rising up to it
fly along the rim

NOLA PASSMORE

RENEWAL

If only renewing the mind
was as easy as renewing a library book.
I could go online,
log into my account,
click the items I wanted to change
and be done.

Positive thinking?
Check.
Wisdom and discernment?
Check.
Sound decision-making?
Check.

But defragging my mind
is harder than the hard drive.
The errors loop on replay,
the screen goes blank,
the system crashes
and I have to start again.

Yet if I listen with my heart,
there's a teacher who's patient,
locates the faults,
reprograms my software,
and enables my macros
to run on
'free'.

I'm ready for my reboot.
Beam me up.
Set me free.

MOLLY PEACOCK

X MARKS HER SPOT WITH LIPSTICK

When X got home from her brush with mortality – just a little
quadruple bypass – she decided that her new heroines would be
exceedingly vigorous and mature despite pesky ailments like heart
trouble. She chose two: one from the afterlife, Diana Vreeland, and
one from among the living, Diana Athill. These exquisite women
were not exempt from death, obviously, but they made the ends
of their lives into excursions, in mind if not in body – artistic,
fashionable, spiritual brief adventures.

Because both Diana A. and Diana V. advised the wearing of makeup in
advanced age, X decided to make a short excursion of her own to an
exclusive makeup counter, one of those exorbitant places that, to her,
was both exhilarating and exhausting. She was determined to try to
exhume a shade of lipstick she'd worn many years ago. Colors always
come back from exile.

Now X didn't want to exaggerate the momentousness of this
adventure, but at the makeup counter she thought she might find the
perfect spot between life and death, the place of x-ing out, the border
crossing, so to speak.

A sparkling young man helped her explore all the different shades,
but she could not find her old fave, Extravaganza, a honey hue. The
best he could do was Xanadu. Just a particle different. Slightly more
evolved. As anything reincarnated into the next level of life would be.

The end of existence, it's just external, isn't it? That's what X now thought.
When one expires, she believed, one simply transforms. One extricates
oneself from human form and starts to become something else. A nice
cloud of ashes to scatter downwind, she hoped, and not in the face of
whoever threw them. Or a nice bit of compost.

Long ago X began to explore the great traditions, those that attempt to explain life and death. As advised by her teachers, she started with Socrates. After she examined what Epicurus and Epictetus had to say (that took her college years), she expended her young woman's energy on the exasperating truths of Buddha. It was only as she aged that they began to make excellent sense to her. Of course, she found ideas about the here and the hereafter in the Bible. And more in the Bhagavad Gita. But so many of the ideas overlapped. Where did they come from, anyway? How did they circulate? They weren't *ex nihilo*. This persuaded her toward reincarnation.

There was a way, she slyly thought, that major ideas were just like minor lipstick colors. They kept circulating, going into exile, so to speak, each an exemplar of a color for a season, and then slightly altered for the next season, and one just waited for them to come back, as if returning from a trip abroad. Ideas were never truly extinct. Take passive resistance, for example. Or even the rotten ones, like misogyny. They seemed to be extinguished, but then they came back! Some thoughts she wished would just exit permanently. (And some colors be extirpated, too.) Yet a person couldn't exorcise them. Even an execrable idea comes back and seems exotic to those who've never experimented with it. Ideas were like stars blinking on and off. Or moon phases.

The night sky excited X – and appalled her. The immensity. The vastness of it. She was so small. Smaller than a sequin. Than a dot. A minim. She was like a molecule. A nanosecond. How could an X mark her spot? What was she worth? Her insignificance used to terrify her. Yet here at the makeup counter, among the many mirrors and the choices of colors whose caps sparkled like the stars, reflecting and refracting, she was. X knew her spot. Right in that mirror. Even though she was a speck, she was a world.

Perhaps, she reasoned, passing out of the mirrored world was like passing into the universe – being exported out there among all the other ideas.

She liked the fact that she was having notions that others had had centuries before, that they somehow were being passed on to her, as if through the air. Inspired by the exhalations of breath from centuries past, she felt strangely secure in a translucent chain of being, each link pale but evident, like shades of moonlight. *Which do I prefer, the sun or the moon?* X asked herself. *Which one, the thing clearly seen – or the thing in mystery?*

'Would you like the Xanadu to replace the Extravaganza?' asked the sparkling young man at the counter.

'I'll try Xanadu,' she replied. 'Let's experiment.' With a mental wave to the living Diana A., she continued on her expedition, crossing the universe (eventually) toward her other heroine, Diana V., and well beyond.

PAUL PERRY

JESUS AS A YOUNG HUNGARIAN DEAF WOMAN CIRCA 1940

The windows were tiny and the train started.
At night the train stopped.
We got off.

We lay down in a huge yard.
We received this uniform, put a kerchief on our heads;
Everybody retained their shoes.

It was odd to be bald.
Everybody was very cold.
I got scared because I found some lice.

It was strange.
The other women's legs were swollen.
We were working in the mud,

Sweeping the area in January.
There were officers sitting at a table –
My sister warned me.

Somebody said, 'Don't you like the deaf?'
I said, 'I listen to my sister.'
I was sent out to dig the graves.

I was the 'crier'.
My hands were hurting...
It was cold.

I wasn't strong.
My sister was much stronger than me.
I was digging the graves.

We were fighting.
We stole from each other.
The last grave I dug was my own.

TONY PEYSER

DISORDERS & DEITIES

My autistic son who often
Is at a loss himself
Paused while taking a bath
And seemed to cross himself.

Did I misinterpret that
Hand gesture a smidgen
Or has Jeremy somehow found
A way to get religion?

His access to godlike things
Would have certain gaps.
My wife & I don't attend services
And are devoutly lapsed.

But maybe some bit of belief
Sang to Jeremy like wishes
Perhaps the prestidigitation
Of those loaves into fishes.

The sight of an actual crucifix
Might be a bit too real for him
He doesn't drink wine but communion
Wafers might appeal to him.

Maybe this is something I imagined
Maybe it's a serious phase
Or just proof that autism & the Lord
Work in mysterious ways.

JAMES POLLOCK

SAILING TO BABYLON

I sailed a boat to Babylon
and rowed back lonely in the rain.
I struck out down a country lane,
I set my course for Avalon,

but once I'd crossed the Acheron
and slept beside the silver Seine,
I sailed my boat to Babylon
and rowed back lonely in the rain.

I've worshipped at the Parthenon,
I've loved the girls of Aquitaine,
but when they lay my bones in Spain,
O tell the Tetragrammaton
I sailed my boat to Babylon
and rowed back lonely in the rain.

BETHANY POPE

THE MINISTER

In essential things my father will only go so far,
Never speaking beyond a certain acceptable,
Credible depth. As children he told us of
Real events I transcribed for school, papers ending, 'its tru'.
Even so, he was careful to wrangle the monsters,
Devils inhabiting the flesh-masks of men. These
Incredible traumas he lived through and dreaded,
Babies the size of a bean he baptized by hand, with
Loving would-be mothers weeping and bloody in beds. I
Expect such stories estranged him from all of us.
How could he sleep with a brain brimming with memories of
Obscene skin-slip warping the features of the
Wounded, born-dead thing he saved for Alpha-Omega?
In essential things, my father will only go so far.

PHOEBE POWER

EASTER WINDOWS

They began blue, greyblue,   aquamarine
and said, take, eat, this is my body
chapel   light   but the night was shadow
unto a place called Gethsemane
window squares   darkened to ink
and he went out, and wept bitterly
where the crucifix hung among stained glass
departed, and went and hanged himself
deepened as the text progressed, slowly
they spit upon him, and took the reed, and smote
edges absorbed   into the glassdark
vinegar to drink, mingled with gall
like a stain seeping blacker, plummets
the ninth hour… Eli, Eli, Lamasabachthani!
sublimates,   till it altogether lost shape

ROBERT PRIEST

TESTAMENT OF A NEW FAITH

as soon as you give birth to a faith
you must begin to heap scorn on it
defile and despise your faith
heap all the world's filth on it
fill it up with stains from the worst acts
of mankind
degrade and abuse your temple
make it the slaughterhouse, the hospital
put your faith through the morgue
let your faith house even the murdered dead
and when you come at last to tear it down
for a failure

if it still stands
if the stone is white underneath
if you wash it off
and it still shines in the sun
with an untempered divinity
then you have a Faith
such as I have

CONCETTA PRINCIPE

HOLD

she tried to change the orbit of the world

wrapping the rosaries 'round it like a chain-link fence, warding off
astral nightmares crashing through the walls

linking roses
a mystic vest against invasions

wearing the chain-link down to fool's gold

there is nothing gentle in the world

sometimes her lips fell apart like petals
in the wind, that was good

the effort of human sweat rusting metal day after day
was not that hard

contemplating nothing more except the desperate hope that
the message was received by something, answering

hold this

MEL PRYOR

FROM GOOD WOMAN

Her severed left breast
loosened its fluids
into a white enamel bowl.

Cross sectioned
it was the agate stone
they stoned her with.

A full cell: del
Piombo, Lanfranco, Karolczak,
Allori up against the oak door.

And Quintiano,
who'd have her body parts
trophied and silvering

among his hunting cups.
Behind the lancet, the haemostat,
the suture's first catgut tug

Agatha's faintful heart,
her ribs agape.
God in the Italian moon,

in the pendulum, the picana,
in the gold star Dog Star's
small burning.

But who was that man
who slipped through the strings
of her iron window,

who held a chalice of milk
to her mouth, bandaged her,
and while she sang

placed his ear to her chest,
listened to the music
of her wounds healing.

LIZ QUIRKE

MNÁ NA HÉIREANN, THIRTY YEARS ON

    and what does it look like
Which names are remembered, what have we learned?
Ann Lovett, Miss Y, Baby X, Miss C
Fallen, scorned, lost and for what?
To cover up, forgive the nameless, blameless Y chromosome
and chasten those who 'couldn't keep their knickers on'

Wheel in the priest, bring out the nuns
Let their novena finally have a function
The worst sinners can't even be churched
Just held up, raised above the pulpit
in a shawl of shame fashioned by congregations
who will happily blaze a sinner's skin

If the spotlight shines between their legs
It can't travel down dim tiled corridors
into rooms where deals are made, papers signed
Not even the moon will illuminate the shapes
of those lurking, low humming cars idling at back doors
waiting to drive fresh born bastards to godly homes

where their crimes and those of their mothers can fade
chip away and burn and the prayerful can rise
reborn with new surnames, installed among the decent
Only afterwards when the embers cool, the air settles heavy
the pious can attempt to wash their hands
cleanse themselves before they kneel to seek salvation

But no running water can remove that handiwork
Soot and ink are tricky tattoos
Once under nails and caked in there's nothing to erase it
You can file the skin perhaps, rub palms with sandpaper
to blur the blackness and at least it can be pretended
that not all hands filled the columns in chapel log books

with only the legitimate, turned pages away
from reports of ill women, raped women and broken girls
ignored by those suited and tied, robed and collared
focused instead on heady pours of altar wine
and decanted back room whiskey left to warm in bellies
swollen, full of a job well done

SUDHA RAO

THE MOTH

night walks in during a rift in your day. after
your torso soaks up the short stark ray-strike.
you halt and glance at the glow bearing down on
the brushed, laden table.
don't stand long and let danger dally
with your measured wing, don't flirt with foolishness.
all is abandoned when the hand moves:
a small spell of time closes in on your night passion.
have you no idea of the coming,
slow, slow sleep? then, hasten your night flight.

SUSAN RICH

THE WORLD TO COME

Let's say we make our own happiness, roll over
in the fields, stain our arms and legs with blue

grass; let's say there's simply one year left
to draw lists of clouds, slip guilt free through bars

of chocolate, hold each other in this black hole
of restlessness. This life.

Tonight we will battle the linoleum squares,
laundry stairs, glass deck where one day

the body is sure to grab its last hungry breath.
What if all that's left for us is gravity,

canned soup, a shimmer of thinning hair?
Let's say we make our own happiness even so —

the tail swoop of katsura trees, triple shots
of strong coffee, a folded map —

Then may I remember to thank the academy
of daily minutiae: suitcases, car keys, a friend's

first novel of karaoke. Who says we can't
have it all: the house of sky and soft catcalls —

Who says we can't find another way
to fail, to come up short, to catch and release.

JAMES RICHARDSON

EVENING PRAYER

How can we blame you for what we have made of you,
war, panic rulings, desperate purity?
Who can blame us? Lord knows, we are afraid of time,
terrible, wonderful time, the only thing not yours.
Granted, we heard what we wanted to hear,
were sentenced, therefore, to our own strange systems
whose main belief was that we should believe.

You, of course, are not religious, don't need any rules
that can be disobeyed, have no special people,
and since a god, choosing (this the myths got right),
becomes human, avoided choices
in general, which is why there is Everything,
even imagination, which thinks it imagines
what isn't, an error you leave uncorrected.

The rumour you were dead, you, I think,
suggested, letting us go with only Pray
into what you had made. By which you meant,
I know, nothing the divine accountants
could tote up on their abaci click click,
but to widen like a pupil in the dark.
To be a lake, on which the overhanging pine,
the late arriving stars, and all the news of men,
weigh as they will, are peacefully received,
to hear within the silence not quite silence
your prayer to us, Live kindly, live.

ROBIN RICHARDSON

WE'RE JUST BEASTS WITH BIG BRAINS

Tipsy on the stoop beside a stone dog, faithful as the hurricane
    that claimed his face. It's okay. The sidewalk's arching orange
towards a chanting patch of shrubbery; it chants your name.
    Or does it state the ways of gods, or god, or something worse?
I have misread myself for years: open as an infant crow below the
worm.
    At my feet some German Shepherd, older than his owner, begs
to be embraced. He has your face. I don't trust this path,
    how cogent its ascent, how calm. I trust the tangle of its swan:
her skyward glance a spire, wingspan something one could
worship
    under, blundering as one does in new idolatry.

CLEA ROBERTS

SPRING SNOWFALL, MELTING

Birds fly up at my feet,
their plain feathers working the air,
and against the blue sky they are a string
of beads thrown from an open window.
An apology of grass lifts itself
through the sacrament of snow as if to say
it's better to leave on good terms,
or saying nothing is lighter than the touch
that awakens, or saying love breathes
best when elevated in the bones
of trees outside our bedrooms,
where we always wake somewhere
different from where we fell asleep.
There is a child at my bedside
stroking my cheek – I did not ask
for this blessing. There is the bright dust
that we breathe. It will take the shape
of anything, furring it with light.

MICHAEL SYMMONS ROBERTS

HOW LONG, O LORD, WILL YOU LEAVE THEM?

Big blond dogs on chains wound
round the wrists of bodyguards;

those chains are made of habit now,
not steel. The curs are going nowhere,

slumped like leather coats with yellow
button eyes. Their handlers *who is*

handling what? wear hooded tops
like dog skins. Ex-bouncers, gangsters,

gatekeepers well past their best
sip sweet strong coffee under broken

street umbrellas. Their lines are episodic,
memory an archipelago of half-

remembered moments in a blank sea.
Estuary, not sea, yes, it is headed somewhere.

Offer them a chaser with the coffee
and they roll tobacco in a note

of worthless currency: '*I used to be…*'
they say '*… the muscle at the gates*

of paradise'. They do not mean the club.
'*Flame, blade, majesty, I had it all*'.

They never mention wings, now tucked
inside their shirts like tattered fans.

Their dogs replay in sleep the day
the world caved in: the exodus, the rush.

Behind their flickering eyes a blaze of skin,
of hide, pelt, breath, a giving way, *a fall.*

JOHN ROE

LAMININ

Sceptics would glower
if I said that Laminin forms
the sign of a cross:
my cross;
it glistens like a feisty jewel,
numbs my senses
speaks peace to my angst and
smells like wild strawberries;
tangy as lemons.
It sparks revelation or provokes a
joke, as you look through the logic.
Dell dwells on its proteins,
as sweet as Indies' sugar:
a beguiling kind of variant.
The truth of its power
can be better.
That cruciform shape
mirrors a black hole,
as meteors laugh and shout
in the universe.
'Morons' say the scoffers,
as Tiger Moths sway
like cobras.
'These "born agains" are dangerous'
say the professors,
'they're a few pennies
short of a sixpence...'
the crackpots see angels
in a piece of oak,
try to ritualise the relic.
'The vilified' are deadly serious,

debunk heresies as leaking cisterns.
Yet the over devout grow blue
in their veins, look on in anguish.
Some day the scientists
will grow tired of warped parables
and quantum equations,
finding truth in a child's
silly play pranks.
God makes humans and
dirty rats, please distinguish,
O Sacre Coeur;
for even as I speak
a donkey sings:
for he will extol
the virtue of Laminin.

ANTOINETTE VOÛTE ROEDER

WHO IS GOD NOW?

Earth
    the green-blue beauty of it

Rain
    the drops, the spaces in between,
    the times when it does not
    rain.

Wind
    when it blows, storms, rages,
    when it lies down in quiet
    pools

Body
    when it rises strong and free,
    entwines with another, when
    it loses its lustre, begins the
    long descent

Love
    in all its facets: birthing, growing,
    breaking, yearning, losing,
    dying

Who is God now?

    Far and near.
    Here, not here.
    Always, all ways
        God.

JANET ROGERSON

INTERVIEW WITH A BELIEVER

I don't doubt it at all, no.
Why do you even ask that?
Do I have the fossilised appearance
of a doubter?
It's like saying the end of the street
is not a sacred place,
or worse, saying it is and then
building a shop there.
No, I don't care if people
think I'm crazy, what does that
mean to me, my skin and heart
reject such labels. Like a can of soup
is labelled with lies, what it says
on the outside, tomato, isn't
a tomato on the inside. It's not
a tomato! Or substitute mushroom,
if you prefer. Your questions
won't pierce me, you should
ask yourself some questions,
then listen carefully for the answers,
though you won't find them,
not where you will be looking.
Why do I believe? [laughs]
Only you can answer that.

PADRAIG ROONEY

SHOWER

When my neighbour waters her geraniums
the drops come down through wisteria leaves
to the level of my balcony where I write
and early morning sunshine catches their fall
onto long thin seedpods that sway so vigorous
and plentiful they have a mind of their own
to become plosive one of these mornings
and scatter their seed all over the garden
and after that velvet touch the stray drops
land in an earthenware pot of seedlings
quickening in new light and seeming to turn
their tender young leaves to face this shower
falling out of nowhere onto this page.

BOB ROSENTHAL

#6 FROM ELEVEN PSALMS

I am child   wanting your all
I give you my fears   my need for instruction
want of material warmth   my love is absolute need
you cut your words into the hands of man   yet you are
not word
words are the voice   empty without melody   strong in
heavens
where song mixes with wind   turns the universe
                        calendar of heaven bound bodies

Daddy please turn your face   hand on my shoulder
let me search the cavern of your deep ear   echoing praises
if I knew you better   I would give up all   all this barking
I would bring my babies to the altar   I would sever my
own tongue
my cries louder still   my heart roasted whole

chasing voices is my avocation   but your voice is the
only one
to gain all your love is to let go my own
Daddy knows but he's gone   let me pry his chords free
let me sing pure Daddy love stronger than offal decay
warmer than addiction mellifluous as bird song over the
power plant

my needs are in shut down   I gift the vowels to you
I'll sleep on hard consonants   I promise this whisper has no
end

JEROME ROTHENBERG

I AM THAT I AM

I am that I am
the god trills.
(He is no more a god
than I or you.)
We see his little boats
ride to the shore
& watch our fathers
like our children
muscle through the waves.
There is a cry
like anybody's
in my throat.
There is a crowd
that fails to see
how our flesh flakes off.
All eyes discern me
where I fall.
No one demands
the tribute
that I cast aside.
I cannot bear it
when they foul my nest.
All that I keep
from those who
sleep beside me
is the calculus of
who they are.
I scorn old people &
discount their days.
I add the numbers
to the newly born

without a thought of
how or why.
I puzzle my old
ways & hide
my fecklessness.
Today is Saturday
forever.
The book is ending
where the book
began.

SARAH ROWLAND JONES

THE CALLING

I'm afraid, she said,
afraid that if I really listen
to whatever God might say
he'll tell me
to go to China
as a missionary.
But I'm nearly seventy,
and my husband has Parkinson's.
And what about my grandson
with learning difficulties
and the neighbour's shopping?

In my unguarded moments
the persistent whisper comes:
no word of China,
just the seducer's unceasing summons
to elope
here
now
without moving an inch.

THADDEUS RUTKOWSKI

SERENITY PRAYER

O Serene One, take away my jitters, so that I may nest like
a bird on a calm ocean, like that mythical bird, the one
transformed by another god, a god different from Yourself,
the bird that was transformed from a grieving widow named
Halcyon, metamorphosed to perch on a circle of sticks on
calm waters so she could be near her drowned husband, to
perch there and lay her eggs, incubate them and help with
the hatching of the chicks, all without leaving the surface
of the sea, without being blown away by wind or rain, this
condition is I all I ask, O Calm One, because I think that a
storm is coming, and that I will be swept away, as if by a very
large broom, and I don't want that to happen, no, all I want
is cool running, just for a while, until I have reached the zen
zone, and after a few minutes there, I'll leave my nest on the
waters, maybe even return home, as if transformed again – a
very rare occurrence, I know – this time from bird to human,
and do human things, like weaving tapestries and such, and
sleep with dreams that are not nightmares about shipwrecks.

OMAR SABBAGH

BETWEEN TWO WORLDS

Dragonfly,
From whom are you exile?

The green gauze of your gazing eye's
Many fingers, like this, here, my
Showboating style...

And so I ask,
In the pink tongue's rhetoric,
Of whom are you terrified,
To whom
Are you terrific?

For you inhabit two riving worlds
And have a bulky heart
With a skinny skeleton of legs.

Out of death, you seem
To quiver, quiver and say: art,

Its mud-brown dregs,
Its rip, rupture, tear
From all the flagrant tares —

The fuel,
A vanishing, a vanishing
Like sweeping tears —

A clash and a duel
Between the mundane and the mulish

And what use you make, what stitch
You stitch
From a God, a before, a beyond,
Effortless, dear, rich

And without qualm,

A mammoth match lit,
A giant hug and slot and fit

Of what's numberless (though at risk),

Ensconced, sat, fixed
On the long and soft divan of love.

EVA SALZMAN

PRACTISES

We all have our peculiar rituals.
I'll be burning every unseen letter
until the neighbours phone the firemen.

There isn't any smell of meat or food,
no sign of skewers of the literal kind.
So when they come, how will I explain myself?

A petty, coward's version of Joan of Arc
where I don't burn, but only all the words
I'd rather see as cinders and as ash?

Or the pagan in me lusting, burning Guys,
celebrating when at last his head explodes
with fireworks – this is one I like!?

Better, candles floating in a bath,
enough of them to make a church of loss
and I'm just supplicant to scent and water.

Better, torch processions on the shore
signalling to someone how the living burns
even though, apparently, anything I burn

will never reach the far-off you: you,
the one I'm burning all these pages for.
When you come, how will I explain myself?

FIONA SAMPSON

SNOW BLINDNESS

He descended into Hell…

Kyrie

At the point of exhaustion
a mind strains

to make things out
This is the vista negativa –

between one blink and the next
colour and detail

are erased
Now thinking

is like climbing –
enormous weights

toll
in the cold air

with the incoherence
of dream

Credo –

That the Christ
is a calving berg –

that He is broken
into being

That He floats on a sea
in sunset calm

the water transparent
and empty

That He is thunder
and wrong chance –

the crack and groan
in the night –

That He is not theft but thief

Gloria

In Simon's photographs the iceberg
is half-pink half-blue –

incongruous delicacy
like the touch of some man on the brink of age

when he strokes your cheek
Incongruous too that this heaped-up mineral pile

seems to suffer and age
as image by image

it shrinks and darkens
in the dark, dirty water off Labrador

where Simon must have tipped about
in some diesel-leaking skiff

his eye, his lens, fixed on the character-full
impersonal ice

That intractable companion
was like being loved

Sanctus

Blessed glop when crushed ice makes water
blessed the ooze and give of slush

Blessed the yoghurt frozen
in ice-cube trays by Barbara's mum

in her formica-and-steel kitchen
at the front of the house

and blessed our games of pirates
on the coal-bunkers out back

Blessed are those sing-song games
of childhood

and blessed the mariners
of the convoys beached

at the bottom of the deep blue
Arctic sea —

Agnus Dei

Late snow buries the lanes
under ten-foot drifts

and tractors stiffen in barns
Up on the edge

the ewe sleeps in her ice-house
The lamb that leaps in her womb

will be born
and he will die

ROBYN SARAH

A PRAYER FOR PRAYER

God! I am dead empty.
Pour me full again.
I am leaden; lighten me.
My cables are cut.

Pour me full again,
a freshly brimming cup.
My cables are cut.
Oh, hook me up!

A freshly brimming cup,
sunstruck, flashing sun's fire:
oh, hook me up,
string me like a lyre

sunstruck, flashing sun's fire,
by this wintry window.
String me like a lyre
and let the hours pluck,

by this wintry window,
a tune from taut gut.
Oh, let the hours pluck
a psalm: forsake me not!

A tune from taut gut:
I am leaden; lighten me.
A psalm: *Forsake me not,*
God! I am dead empty.

DENISE SAUL

HOUSE OF BLUE

There is something detached
about this colour which stands
for the sky. It contains
everything and yet nothing.
At the House of Blue (which takes
its name from that music, the Blues),
I rattle the sistrum until the villagers
run from the prayer-house to see
the clouds above Lake Tana.

They discovered when I was almost
seven, that I could make rain fall
whenever I played the sistrum.
That year, the farmers looked
at books and magic scrolls
to read the weather.
The local herdsman threw
a bucket down a well
and heard it hit the bottom.

It was not far from here –
at the brazier's shop – where
the smith pounded out a piece
of copper on his anvil.
Once I listened to the pitch
between notes made by metal
and hammer, I returned
to the House of Blue and carved
a sistrum handle from acacia.

At intervals, I attached five
discs to each of the traverse wires.
When I played *Apocalypse
of Gregorios* or *Song of Baruch*
and added blue notes,
the discs jingled together.
I even noticed that the first
sound was twice as long
as the second.

Think of a barley field,
when a woman plants
seeds for next summer,
she sits on the grass to take
possession of the earth.
The need for water stops her
listening to what is
happening in this village.
Note the breeze that carries
husks across the stream-bed
while the same plough
rests in the yard.

LESLEY SAUNDERS

STILL LIFE (WITH LEMON)
after the painting by Willem Claeszoon-Heda, 1638

Without doubt the lemon
is Christ – look how it's pared
to the quick, an epiphany

of citrus, its glistening sliced
from God's own brightness,
set on the supper table in sight

of the faithless, you and me.
It's His light that breaks and enters,
freeing our sprites of flesh

with a carafe of wine or this fall
of whitened linen, caging angels
in a pane of glass; light portrayed

as pure knife, sheer skill, a whetted steel
to peel your eyes and shred your soul.

RONNIE SCHARFMAN

PRAYER

I have always hoped
that struggling towards You
is You.
But I am never
sure.
And that is, perhaps,
You, too.

In Jabès's admonition
to 'preserve the question'
is the ray of light
the chorus of voices
the shelter of connection
the anchor of the centuries.
Yet, is also the abyss
the receding shore
the vertigo of the depths.

JACOB SCHEIER

ODE TO THE DOUBLE RAINBOW GUY

It's starting to look like a triple rainbow! Oh God! What does this mean? – Paul Vasquez

You lost your shit over shades of light
or as you proclaimed, oh my god
a double rainbow all the way –
and were received like all our prophets,

with scorn. Too filled with emotion to reflect
tranquility, you burst into tears
which from some odd angle
made a small rainbow, somewhere.

Oh god, oh my god, you spoke like Job
in reverse, suddenly seeing that we'd
been given everything, and asked
god, what does this mean?

We answered you with laughter
because we no longer know
what it means to be astonished.
For this, for everything, we are auto-tuned.

Oh my god, what does it mean
to care about something or someone
that much. Woo! You knew
triple rainbows were impossible.

MICHAEL SCHMIDT

THE RESURRECTION OF THE BODY

…So will I melt into a bath to washe them in my bloode… – S. Robert Southwell S.J.

The cellar floor is swept. Women are weeping
Like shadows in torchlight, around the straw pallet they hover,
The soon-to-be-mourners, a dozen, discarding their shawls,
Unpinning their hair. It's so hot in the cellar of death.
Professional, they know what's to come:
She will shrug, shiver, jaw drop open, let go.

Led out of blinding daylight the Healer comes down.
He raises his hand and stills the scrum of women.
He comes down like a lamp into a cavern,
Gathering from sweltering noon light a cool glow.
He comes as if out of the desert sequinned with dew
And his gaze, austere, not unkind, goes through the women
Settling on the parched form stretched on the pallet,
Human, almost beyond pain, but not a child.
The man did say child but she is almost a woman,
Her delicate feet, long legs, the down at her crotch,
Flat belly, firm, the handsome small domes of her breasts
Panting, panting, not a child, though her father, grieving,
Insists, believing, a child. So he says to her, *child*.

She focuses her dark gaze on his amazing pallor,
Her fever like a bruise against him. She closes her lips
Reaching for a sheet, the rolled winding sheet, for cover
But he makes her calm, she understands, her lips now parted
Rapt, she holds her breath (she has breath to hold now).
She watches him, he bends down to her, to lift her up,
His shirt falls open, she sees where the wounds will be.
What does he feel when he gathers her hot and shivering
Off the pallet, hardly a weight, so smooth, and all

The smells upon her, faeces and stale sweat, the scent
Of her scalp, and her breath quite sweet, a surprise;
That hot smooth flesh, that shit and flowers, urine
And something else; and the haze of down on her arms
Up to the elbows, then the quite smooth darkness,
Substance of shadow, her flesh, so smooth, and the breathing
Not weary or fretful now in that limp body;
What does he feel, seeing his own white arm beneath her dark hair,
When he knows what he holds, and what it does to his legs,
To his groin, his bowels, to his rapid heart? He holds her
And out of his chest where she is pressed against him
Flows that unusual grace which is rooted in muscle,
Which comes from the marrow and lymph, which is divine,
The grace of a man whom love has turned into God,
The love of incarnate God whose flesh knows the name of his creature.
He holds her the way his mother will soon cradle him,
Passion giving life, or love; and then compassion.

And what does she feel? Who can know what she feels?
What you would feel, or I, pressed close to his chest,
To his cool skin, his smell of the dust of the road,
Of hearth fires, of wine, the touch of his hair, of bread...
What does she feel? She feels love, she feels his desire
Confusing her, desire but not need, he holds her
Tenderly, his lips to her shoulder and hair.

Out of the cellar he bears her into the air
Shedding her pestilence and the sun dissolves it.
A crowd has assembled. He walks among the crowd
With his light burden, they watch and withdraw, afraid,
Conjuror, they see the girl gaze in his eyes.

At the well he sets her down, she can stand on her own.
At the well she stands straight as a reed and Jesus bathes her,
First her hair, he pours water from a hollowed gourd,
Then her ears and eyes and lips, her face, her neck,

Her heart and hands, her back, her belly, her long thighs,
He washes her feet as if she were a child.
The fever has passed. She calls him *father, father*
Though the man who is her father stands beside him.
She calls him father. He wraps her in his own shirt.

MYRA SCHNEIDER

CLOUD

Dusk: behind the blurring railway bridge
a row of December roofs is emerging
and long-disused chimneys are stamped

on luminous apricot like repeating
paper cut-outs a child has carefully pasted
into her scrap book. Above tree laceries

a cloud soft as the line of roofs swells into
a scalloped sea animal and glides across
the panes in the bay window. The day's demands

slip from my shoulders as the creature humps
and begins to caterpillar into low islands.
The movement is so slow, so effortless

in what is now an ocean of faintest blue
it seems to be part of the stillness. I wish
I could think that what I'm looking at is heaven;

to people in the seventh century *heofan* and sky
were a single word. I can't believe
the divine exists in a fixed place overhead –

isn't god the energy driving the universe,
the dimensions of its mathematics visible
in patterns on this planet, the union of sperm

and egg, our compassionate connections
with one another, small selves drifting
into the damson wings of darkening clouds?

DAVID SCOTT

A PRIEST AT PRAYER

From prayer to prayer involves
a dwindling, a way of being
that accounts for weariness, a regular
drawing in and letting out of breath;
the planting of a word and its forgetting,
a close examination of what is there
until it isn't, a candle flame beating air,
love meeting Love before the house wakes up;
space body-shaped, time vacated,
the passive tense, a waiting to receive,
out-of-bounds of what is right
or wrong, subject to being surprised
by God on briefest sight.

RICHARD SCOTT

TRAINEE PRIEST AT ROCHUSKAPELLE

Saint Sebastian stands covered with the hunger-cloth –
a hooded detainee from off the seminary television.
We must give up the sight of him to focus on the bare Easter altar.

Good Friday I will lift the veil, search his face for a clue of agony.
I don't believe the sculptor's lie, he cannot be at peace.
He is like me, young when he gave himself to God.

While the priests are diluting wine
I would have him tug off his sack, step down, walk.
I will lie him across my lap, pull out the cock-feathered arrows,

wash the holes in his body, sew them up
with my mother's darning needle, ask if I will be forgiven
for wanting his delicate blood on my fingers.

But Sebastian is carved, I have traced the chisel's evidence
with my thumb. I know my thread can't heal –
he and his arrows are of the same body of Milanese oak.

There is no stop where either wound or weapon begin –
our devotion is a perpetual hurt. I am like him,
young, bound for a lifetime of suffering behind cloth.

REBECCA SEIFERLE

ALBRECHT DÜRER: THE MARTYRDOM OF THE 10,000

That same gaze, looking out of us, out of the vanity
of his hair, out of the black shroud of his figure, the walking
stick in his hand, or is it waving his signature like a flag
of independence... he and his friend, artists, Humanists,
walking through this scene where 10,000 are being
martyred by cardinals in mitres, caliphs in turbans,
all of the religious figures resplendent with their robes
and roles, while those who are being crucified, stoned
to death, or driven off the edge of a cliff like a stampeding
herd of swine are naked, their flesh vulnerable in
a landscape where even the rocks have turned against
them. 'What is he trying to say?' my students ask me,
and I don't know. He had to give human form and story
to the Emperor's collection of relics, Frederick's
knucklebones and splinters of sternums, but
the friend he is walking with, also dressed in black,
was already dead when he started this painting,
so Dürer has painted himself as a man in mourning
walking with a dead man through a killing
field. Perhaps it's some somber lesson he garnered
from his trips to the Vatican, perhaps something
about how art and learning make one independent,
apart, from the age's craze of religious killing, all
those saints and martyrs that he, as artist, was paid
to give the brush to. He is an observer, a witness
perhaps like God, who looks at us, taking our measure
against the lack of humanity in the humanity
of this scene, perhaps he has been driven so far
past what language can say of this, for all of these
killings are driven by language, or perhaps he is like
that anthropologist, who in search of another

wall to break through, turns to
the language of dolphins, and looks back at us,
digging into the shore of a cruel land, with
the questioning, piteous gaze of the sea.

SUDEEP SEN

CHANT

om ma ni pad me hum

blank contains
        everything –

everything contains
        nothing –

nothing contains
        all –

all is one –
        one is many –

many
        is all –

om ma ni pad me hum

DON SHARE

THE GOSPEL TRUTH

St. Matthew did not know that mites live
      in our eyelashes,
or he'd not have indicted us for our
      motes and beams.
Every character in my name a mark
      of resolves, notwithstanding
all I have is a forlorn inclination –
      but even that seems to be bent.
The strips of insulation in the attic hang
      down, flayed and torn.
We need a new border, and ought to poison
      the chickweed before it goes dormant.
Where is he, meanwhile, who will save us,
      wound in his side?
The one who knows is off on another
      job, collecting taxes, impervious
to the indignity of having been reborn.

SANDY SHREVE

QU' APPELLE

That night, there was an inkling in the distance
of auroras; just a hint of colour, pulsing where the heavens
met the prairie's edge. When midnight came,

the palest green began to billow in the distance
while we sang Amazing Grace, a cappella harmonies
enough to break the heart of darkness and make

that night before we left, the distance disappear
as we (barely breathing) watched the heavens bloom.

Qu'Appelle Valley (Saskatchewan, 1999)

MARTHA SILANO

GOD IN UTAH

with apologies to Barbara Ras

As we gossiped at the hotel bar about ex-es and trances,
lechers and facelifts, God in the oil, bathing with the lightly-

breaded scallops, God resting on the bed of squash risotto;
God making sure the mushrooms on our plates didn't kill us.

As we debated coffee or no, God hovered between Hank
and his nametag as he described the peanut brittle compote.

After we laid down our napkins, after we downed the last drops
of Pinot Grigio, God followed me to the ladies, to a back room

where the good people of Salt Lake knocked back Manhattans,
obedient souls in crisp white collars, sensible oxfords. And God

was in the dark where the TV blared through the wall behind the bed,
where the moment the music crescendoed and the credits rolled,

a throbbing toe woke me; God in my left toe, God in the purple pillbox,
God in the ibuprofen that relieved me. I spied God the next morning

in Nikki's nostrils, in Keegan's fading acne, tasted God in my breakfast burrito,
extra chili on the side. On the tour of Temple Square, God cracking up outside

the tabernacle, in stitches over the secret handshakes, especially the Patriarchal
Grip, God in his grandeur guffawing over barring from worship the un-

recommended. God defiantly breaking the rule against unbridled laughter.
God floating from garment to garment, especially those escaping

their clotheslines, drifting over rooftops, finding safe harbor
in a sweet gum or maple. God soaring over the visitor center

in the form of a falcon, but though a glossy pamphlet suggested I reflect
on the majesty of His creations as I stood beneath the star-studded dome,

the outstretched arms of an eleven-foot savior, God could not be detected
in the sound-muffling, dull-beige carpet. God in the breezes from People's

Freeway to Liberty Wells, God in the stratification, all the way down
to the very bottom, two billion year's worth of sandstone, limestone, shale;

God in the volcanoes gracing that geologic layer cake with an ashy frosting;
God in the 85% who live within fifteen miles of the Wasatch Mountains;

God in those who do not; God in the rhyolite, in the granite; God
in the brachiopods and the triops, in the millions of tons of monzonite quartz

hauled from a glacial trough in Little Cottonwood Canyon, where God hangs out
with the one-head sunflower, the everywhere aster.

KATHRYN SIMMONDS

THE VISITATIONS

Sometimes God comes as a tiger,
And sometimes as a rose –
He opens for you secretly,
Perfuming your nose.

Sometimes he is a telephone,
Sometimes he is a key,
Sometimes he comes with hoola hoops,
Sometimes a dictionary.

Sometimes he comes as creosote
And leaves a nasty stain,
Sometimes he comes as anyone
Whose motives you can't name.

Sometimes he comes as sunlight –
Watch him tick across the wall.
And sometimes as a boxing glove.
And sometimes not at all.

FLOYD SKLOOT

LOST PSALM

God was the clear pane at the heart
of a stained glass burning bush
filling the temple's western wall.

God was water when I walked
the beach during the eye
of a hurricane. God was water
swelling as the storm moved
across land and then was
the storm in full force.

God was a dune risen
to meet the surge and God
was a dune shrunk
to welcome winter wind.

God was on the tongue
of the first girl I kissed,
then God was on my tongue.

God spoke with flickering
light in a flood of sighs,
spoke without breath,
warm, spoke in tongues.

God was high in the stands
when I was knocked free
of time and space for one
full week making a tackle
in the open field. I shook
on the ground as if charged

by His light. All next spring
and early summer, God sped
through cycles of color
just beyond the edge of sight.

Doctors named it an aftereffect
of trauma but I understood it
was the afterglow of grace
and for months God could be
glimpsed in the creases of dream,
heard just beyond the bell buoy
at land's end, felt in spindrift
when the moon was full.

Finally God was in eastern
Pennsylvania, looming in books
and seminars. But somewhere
on the Susquehanna near Safe Harbor,
crewing a Flying Dutchman,
stretched out to my fullest
over the rushing river
in an effort to keep us all afloat,
I lost Him in a sudden luff of wind.

TARA SKURTU

INDIAN RIVER AT DUSK

The first and only time I caught a sheephead
big enough to eat, black and white and breathing
in my hands. On my way to get ice I got
distracted, tossed Dad's keys in the water.

I was a good Catholic: I walked him to the spot
and pointed. I made up a lie, but I named
everyone I loved to God before falling
asleep in my yellow room every night –

God was a word person. After two
Hail Marys and an Our Father I'd be
good again. Like my words, I knew where
the keys landed. I've tried to write

about this before. For over a year I made myself
guiltless, couldn't preserve the thing I caught
or get the syntax right. I didn't know about
currents. I can't keep anyone safe.

JESSICA SLENTZ

HOLLOWED BE THY NAME

Stones. Collected, connected and set with
the sweat of slaves and masons' spittle. Clay
mortar, hay bricks, quarried limestone, bedrock
circles, towering isosceles graves,
caves, columns, cloisters, buttresses, busts, saints.
These sacred spaces. This cold density,
bleak monotone chill. Slate grey walls swallow
shards of color, and echo with the hum
of ancient prayers. Fragmented abstractions.
Windows that can never be transparent.
To see through is to see what is outside,
beyond – empty motion, real time, sun glare,
breaking, haze, devotion. To allow light
is to illuminate. To color
is to cloud. These sacred places, solemn.
This ornate mosaic, this creation,
this psalm of reverence built in part to plea
erasure of chaotic frailty.
To ornament humanity. Hone to
resemblance, carve to remembrance, sketch to
illustrate, etch to urn. These gilded domes
and symbols, faded passion plays in stone,
parables in words no longer known. Veils
to step beyond, these tolling bells, these womb
quiet expanses, this silence that is larger
than you.

EDWIN SMET

ELONGATED

I, for one,
have nothing to define the contents
of what seems to be me, let alone
a system which created it all.

I only know, contemplating flyleafs
on hidden speech, monarchs in Mexican
trees, watching sunlight transform
freshly washed hair, reading

solitary pages by Sebald, the gravity
of his voice, the trees again – it all
brings out sufficient matter

how to elongate sensibility,
to poke interest, to find joy
in this distorted divinity.

BARBARA SMITH

TERESA OF THE ECSTATIC UPLIFT

by Bernini: Cornaro Chapel, Santa Maria della Vittoria, Rome

I want to break with gravity's pull,
I crave consummation and mutation.
My folds blow inside out this intense
desire. It's not easy being fixed to this marble cloud
companioned by *that* angel, his loaded
arrow, aware of coins slotting out a light-ray
and who believes this elevated *aedicula?*

Beneath my eyelids is what you want to feel:
fluttering visions rolled up tight, re-arrayed
inside the deep channels of my clothes,
my toes curled in sacred shock, my tongue
slack against my mouth's roof, staggering
eternally for Christ, pulse chilled to stat –
betrayed by the integrity of stone.

The others weren't trying to hold me down
as they grappled the dew on my hem –
each time I rose along the cell walls
my lips mumming long prayers,
ears tuned to some unknown colour
far beyond the high severity of Avila –
no, they were trying to rise with me.

Somebody succeeded though,
in marbling ecstasy in deep creases.
Someone knew how to make my habit
textual, how to make coarseness
fresh and how to leave me *dressed* –
my face, hands and feet polished slick,
my spirit effusing from the erogenous zone.

V.A. SOLA SMITH

HIM

When I say I am not religious
you tell me to pray to god
as I understand him.

Not *her*. Not *it*. Not the idea.
Him – the very reason I cannot,
I will not put my hands up.

Why consent to be nailed to a cross?
Why float my worth in unknown waters?
Why must I give my prayers up to *Him*?

After all, *I am*
not asking for a miracle.
Yet, *you*, who is –

why do you choose to believe
you cannot help me?
You could so easily

just confess
you are, and so be
the miracle I need.

ROSE SOLARI

A PRAYER

Learn to love the square
of sky you see each night
through the cloister window.
Let it stand for all
the world you cannot
have, and love that, too.

ELIZABETH SPIRES

CONSTRUCTING A RELIGION

After Larkin

Not the rising sun,
but the setting sun.
Not the father,
but the mother.
Not the cross,
but the circle,
drawn in ink,
not blood.

The Word
inhabited
but unspoken,
like a bell unrung.

A cathedral
of the mind,
grey and cool
as Time,
with doors
so tall and heavy
that I must
tug and tug.

Inside, marvels
and terrors
annealed in
bright windows,

and a bird
sheltering in
high hidden spaces,
looking down

on a soul,
small, so small,
prostrate
on stone.

FRANCES SPURRIER

GOSPEL PASS

High where the rain is glass
and the sky overburdened with cloud,
Gospel Pass
winds its way
through the black hills of Wales.

The crusaders passed this way, they say
resting the rough wooden cross against a rock
as they carried it
from Llantony Priory to Hay
or offered it up at Capel-y-Ffin.

I will lift up mine eyes...
There are places where you don't want to look down.
There are places you don't want to leave
yet leave you always do,
while the mountain batters
        with its hailstorm breath
        renders inarticulate
the heart as sound as stone.

JOHN STILES

I'M NOT SHY YOU KNOW

I'm not shy, you know.
I'm not a saint, you know.
I just go there,
in the air,
you know?
I like to sit, in the back, writing
things, seeing things, thinking things,
you know?
I have chemistry,
you know?
With a few that
I know.
I've seen Angels,
I see it all.
From the back, in the train cars,
under signs, under lamps,
getting bumped,
gasping at people,
you know?
Testing ways I go on my instinct
waiting for what?
I heard it all – spirituality is wrong...
No. No. No. I don't think so.
I don't think so.
Y'know?

CHLOE STOPA-HUNT

HARBOUR-CHAPEL

And I have asked to be / Where no storms come – Gerard Manley Hopkins

What light is, what vessel,
What heart is.
Coming to harbour, the flaking cherry tree bent
To kiss, and to sorrow for the heart
Of the thin-winged swallow Percival buried once,
None can forget it,
For the hart that Gawain scared,
Her burnt grey sobs.
We all decode our blows: *what light is,*
What vessel, what heart is.

LIANE STRAUSS

THE PIANO TUNER

You have to understand, it wasn't like it is today.
Back then there was the war and we believed in miracles.
Roosevelt was like a god, immortal.
And a visit from the piano tuner was an event,
looked forward to like Santa Claus here in America,
or a trip to the theatre.

In our family of musicians, no one ever touched Lolly's piano.
It was unspoken but forbidden.
Secretly, my sister and I longed to play it.
It rose up in the corner like a black iceberg.
Opened for company: our Phantom Archaeopteryx
of folded wing and broken song.
The casket closed, it was austere as any tomb,
even the name in mother of pearl
laid like a pale flower on its chest, down to the umlaut.

Until the day one of the aunts pulled out the bench,
sat down and produced the hysterical uproar that made us jump
like Hic Haec Hochdeutsch on our new RCA Victor.
And that's how it came about
that we were expecting a visit from the piano tuner.

For weeks my sister and I could think of nothing else.
He would come and everything would be altered.
We had such romantic ideas.
He would come and tune the piano to ourselves,
turn us and our wide-eyed passion all to music.
We lay awake in a state of expectation
like Dante's souls in limbo, or the children of Hamelin.

On the morning of the day of his appointment
my sister and I could hardly eat.
We were almost sick with anticipation.
In a dream, the clock struck the hour and the doorbell sounded.

But oh the creature who entered the front parlour!
He was half blind, with a squint, dwarf short, half lame
and he limped, which he somehow hid. And the tools
he dug up, pawing in his dead leather satchel,
were neither old nor worked, and he handled them
without a trace of tenderness.
And then the grovelling way he blinked,
rolling his head off at a crazy angle,
and the thick noises that came from his chest,
which made us think he might just turn and spit
on the parquet or ruin the antique Persian carpet.
And the furtive clicking in his throat before he spoke.
And the accent not too far from Father's.
And the tick tick tick of metal buttons at the wooden panels.

Afterwards there was no real reason to steer clear.
No one even called it Lolly's piano.
My sister and I had our weekly lessons.
Every evening, after schoolwork, we took turns and practiced.
But it never sounded absolutely right.
Maybe it was the acoustics in the parlour.

And sometimes, just like that morning, even now,
I see the piano tuner, the bad leg of his trousers
hitched, the body riven from its lid, and hear
the sickening sound of tone moving
as he gobbles his tongue, rummages,
peering over the side, in his con doctor's kit,
goring the dark innards, the dirty fingers of his fist
coiled about the shabby silver-plated idol,
as the piano, like an animal submitting,
turns to me its dull, unblinking eye of death.

SEÁN STREET

ISENHEIM

Altarpiece, Matthias Grünewald Musée D'Unterlinden, Colmar

Before there was art history,
there was a collaboration.
Saint Anthony's inmates aghast
saw the hospice god manifest
in their image out-staring them,
a dying they could understand.

Aesthetics – very easy when
your skin isn't bursting open.
For all we rationalise it
through a curtain hung with hindsight
from the current summit, this art's
just a painting without their pain.

But it's as close as we get now,
graced with our definitive eye,
long generations' honed wisdom.
So *Isenheim*, face me down,
share all of that distant witness
beyond a cross to a likeness.

MELISSA STUDDARD

OM

He sent us flowers without a card,
God did – that trickster soul.
It must have been a sound that started it all,
and he's still out there somewhere, laughing
while we seek directions, or direction,
while we, the addressees, search for an addresser,
while we sort and sift and categorize and collect,
divide, classify and analyze. Our refrigerators hum to us,
and heaven knows the bugs make their merry at night.
Once I even saw the color yellow hum
when I imagined Van Gogh stroking its thick,
vibrant passion onto the page.
That yellow song was anything but hum-drum.
I swear, I felt it on the roof of my mouth
and at the back of my throat
like a yogic ritual or some sort of Tantric stunt.
Even deep in my chest, yes, I felt the hum.
And in the other room – the clothes in the washer,
round and around they went, their own spinning universe,
and next to them, a parallel world, the dryer,
connected to the same outlet,
hum, hum, humming away.
This life is anything but ho-hum,
with all this motion and noise.
Hell, I can hardly even hear over the hum of my phone,
which I have cursed for interference,
which I have indignantly labeled, 'that silver piece of shit,'
which I have threatened to replace (like it cares),
and which was really Om all along.
Washing clothes, I've since learned, is an act of prayer.

COLE SWENSEN

THE GHOST STORY

began as a collision   between what the Church said   and what everybody saw
in the sky between   the trees if a cloud   could have taken on

legible form   you could have lost your way   it could have followed you home

And so the concept of a ghost was itself   something that returned   that drifted back
from an earlier system of belief   for had it been known that the dead are not at peace

what would Christ have said   had held   his children in a silver fever for the voyage
to death was a bridge and not a river   with a gate that swings   one way in patient only

one lonely moment in which   if the moment falters, alters   you almost sever
but the Church fathers could never   quite convince them of this

MARGO SWISS

MOTHER GOD

Thus He is our mother…and He wills that we know this,
for He will have all our love fastened to Him.
Julian of Norwich, *A Shewing of God's Love*

On hands and knees before you, God, I fall,
bear with grief this wretched beggar love.
Face down dead I lay
the once soft heart You worked in me,
turned now so sickly hard,
that hardening harder still
is doomed to kill
my light and life.

The sin I bring devours my rest,
eats and burns within
yet wears itself without
by such disguise as otherwise
seems meet and right.

How shall I find You now, O Saviour God,
in this dry parching heat?
A desert land extends no hand to spare
what further shame I fear:
your mighty rod that reigns
to break the back of my desire
to be your constant child.

Become, dear Christ, instead, my Mother God.
Exchange this brutal love that bends
for one that raises up,
that You, once soiled for me,
shall call this breach a necessary sin

to lead me home
and by my own
poor nakedness in You
redress your glory, Lord.

MARIA TAYLOR

MY UNCLE'S CREED

I heard my uncle's low-slung notes
before I saw him. A feral litany of bass
pulsing through the grey paving slabs
of Kentish Town. Since he'd given up
on a son and wedlock, it seemed that God
had marked him for a book of psalms.

His eyes scraped across his set face
to look inside the mirror of my own,
but he'd refused to speak, since I married
an *englezo*, so he passed, contriving to groan
Jesus Christ, the saints and the Holy Spirit,
aided by a gargle of communion wine.

He headed towards his wifeless maisonette,
liturgies thrumming with the shoddiness
of all mankind, each vowel pouring like lava
with God slurred in a burning *Kyrie Eleison*.

N.S. THOMPSON

SILENT MESSIAH

He hung there limply on the frame,
His body beaten black and blue.
Exposure was the thing; humiliation, too;
To which the nails seemed superfluous
When all you had to do was die of shame;
Quietly expire, a minimum of fuss.
But what a noise you made, Silent Messiah,
Your humbling death, so nakedly exposed,
Conquered forum, basilica and the choir
Of poets with the love you interposed.

RÓISÍN TIERNEY

THE PACT

Jesus, she said she was pure!
But when I saw her belly swelling
I knew I had to act and fast.
We held the wedding in the Palace of Bells.
That kept the neighbours quiet.
I never asked who or why
and she never volunteered
any information. We'd always been mates
you see. We had an understanding.
I'd look out for her, and she for me.
Then one day I heard her talking to the sky,
and knew I'd lost her. She was looking upwards,
hands fluttering, and kept saying the same words over:
'The stoning, not the stoning'.

RACHEL TOBIN

PRAYER OUTSIDE A CONFESSION BOX

bless me, great spirit, i have sinned:
i have knelt a lifetime at another altar
and this is my prayer.

i lay down the argument
ironed to the hem of my heart
that i am judge of what is just and fair.

i lay down the anger i was born without embrace
begat by a man who broke in horses and the spirit of children.
i lay down the rage *that i succumbed*.

i lay down the belief that because one man i called
my lover, was street-shoes careless with this heart,
i am not good, desirable or loving enough.

i lay down the strangling waves of snake that rise,
the knife questing blood because it cuts,
the white-hot critic because acid burns.

i lay down my demand for apology, for acknowledgment.
i lay down the words i've shaped, like scorpions, to punish.
i lay down my steel-gold insistence the other caused this pain.

i lay down my determination to feel abandoned
because the truth says i am never abandoned
and i want to see how moon is blue.

i lay down the anger that *you* have not been on *my* side.
i lay down the need for anyone to understand.
i lay down the belief i'm the only one who's been to hell.

i lay down the thought that others are better.
i lay down wanting something other than the *now*,
even though it's bitter, and stings.

and most of all i lay down the belief
that i am any other than a wild-goated woman
with songs strong enough to open your heart

and mine, with fire enough to topple tables
in the temple of my own betrayal.
i scatter these judas coins skyward;

i lift my face from the gravel, blood and sting
of self. i absolve myself from my sins
without a glory be in sight,

with no allegiance to any other
than *you* in *me*.
and so it is.

SAMUEL TONGUE

MORNING

Sometimes what people mean by faith
is the ability to believe
in the sheer impossibility
of morning and the way

things happen outside ourselves
even before we wake.
An unseen cat scampers across
a slick river of cold concrete.

A blackbird opens an orange rimmed eye
and sings. Streetlights flick off suddenly
leaving a slow afterglow of night

and, as the milk builds up on the doorstep,
someone receives a letter
giving him another reason to live.

HELEN TOOKEY

THEN IS IT TRUE

Aber weil Hiersein viel ist, und weil uns scheinbar alles das Hiesige braucht, dieses
Schwindende, das seltsam uns angeht… – Rilke, 'Ninth Elegy'

Then is it true, that you also need us?

Look: here, at this angle of land, where riverbank
becomes coast, here is salt ice lying

in the furrows, and there, where water
exchanges with water a mode

of being, river/ocean/river, there
again is ice, thin-skinned and scarcely

bearing, puzzling rocks; and the cold,
to us, is like a new live thing, that stalks

the hollows of our bones. – Look: I am
giving it to you, this fragment; but how,

in your completeness, could you need it?

ANGELA TOPPING

CRADLE CATHOLIC

For years I dreamed of leaving
but the pull was strong: so many
memories of being moved and loved,
of lit candles and swelling organ music,
bright words glittering.

As holy bells warned us to raise
bowed heads, adore, we'd chant
Glory, glory, glory, Lord God of Hosts.
On long walks home from church,
I'd mither for the words of hymns
before reading unlocked my first poetics.

What gorgeousness was there?
The year's calendar shone in vestments:
silks of purple, green and white
embroidered with gold thread
by cloistered nuns, the stitches prayers.
Words like *ciborium* and *monstrance*,
biretta and *stole*, delighted the ear.

Incense mingled with damp wool.
The congregation intoned as one:
lamb of God, ave, womb –
a mysterious place our Lord came from.
I thought it meant the sound of voices
moving together like water.

The round bread, baked by holy sisters,
was God's eye, scouring secret hearts.
The priest placed it on stuck-out tongues
where the wafer slowly melted.
The palate's ribbed roof was tabernacle.

Angels clustered round the altar. I thought
I could hear their wing beats. I offered
all my sorrows up to Jesus, as I'd been taught.
But this was my mother's God. Without her
I had to find my own ways of knowing.

ALAN PATRICK TRAYNOR

THE EYES THAT DRANK THE TREES

I am the dandelion
The soul of God

So tread on me carefully
As the ecocide
As the earwig knows

I am the ecliptic
The hand buried diamond
And I am blowing erratically

The thread that hurried time
Becomes the rock!

I am carefully moaning
And I am drinking of you
The reflection that is woman
Oh blurry walk

A reflection of time
And delicacy
That twists
I drank the trees

The elflock
That hurls
The child's hair
Viridian

I am your soul
In pieces

ROBERT VAS DIAS

EPIPHANOUS

Becoming or arriving is the nature of Khepri…
But every arising occurs in and from death,
which thus appears to be potential life. *

Above the tourist tat and toiletries
perched on a dusty top shelf:
carved granite *kheper* —

scarab-beetle, he who rolls dung-balls
along the ground, buries them,
from which baby *kheper* arise

miraculously. Hence Great Khepri,
he who comes into being, who
daily wheels sun-disk across hot sky

over the horizon to that other
place beyond. *Kheper* emerges from
puff of *Duat* dust, came into being

by artisan's toil with mallet and chisel,
pounder and maul, bow and awl
revealing the shape living within

solid speckled Aswan granite.
He coldly, stonily stares, at me alone
he stares, this dry, dead, stone.

Is his warmth the sun's or does my blood
quicken it? My hands cradle, caress it.
Behold, make a scarab of green stone —

or Aswan granite – *and place it*
in the heart of a man and it will perform
for him the 'opening of the mouth'

in that other place, that other life,
so he may speak forever
interceding with the living.

* W.B. Kristensen, quoted by N. Rambova in A. Piankoff, 'Mythological Papyrus: texts,'
in Bollingen Series XL.3, Pantheon Books, 1957, pp.29-30, in George Hart, *Egyptian Myths*,
London, British Museum, 1990, p. 53.

JANET VICKERS

ALMIGHTY FACILITATOR

May we address you, from now on, in second person
instead of third person?

May we address you with our quiet reflections
instead of praying for personal favours?

May we learn to trust your silences as our time out
for behaviour that is not so much a sin
against you as the way we have lost?

May we develop a relationship
feeling your arms like wind and music
around us

(we are here for such a short time)?

Please forgive us for imposing our face upon you
expressing our desires as your will
for speaking on your behalf

and

Dear Creator
may we learn very soon
that your promise to make the world
a place the meek shall inherit
is really our task and the reason
you gave us metaphors
and stories.

Blessed be.

VAL VINOKUR

YOUR WORSHIP

I am your pilgrim, who wanders
to stay home; your monk,
who keeps silent when you demand
confessions and theology.
You are too difficult to love
directly; you have no roof
or floor, and I am too pious
for your rain and mud.
So I keep your shrine, the best of you,
the clean, the singing rest of you.
I am a stubborn priest, who knows himself
only in the dwindling oil of you,
the weeping and rebellious flame
about to die.

G.C. WALDREP

COMMON PRAYER

Prayer is a harrow. No iambs or incentives, no cherubim, no majuscule illumination. The hero stirs from his bed of the mind, blinks in drowsy sunlight. The risk of talking to God is that He may talk back, or else remain silent.

The forest is not a biddable place. Comes the harrow.

Beloved, whispers the paper birch, and then continues in its insensible tongue. We, rapt, grasping at its supple branches, choose to hear *Beloved, beloved, beloved*.

The logic of dryad, of hamadryad is speech into speechlessness.

Prayer says: beneath this birch a soldier once executed a prisoner with whom he had been charged, because he did not wish to be inconvenienced on his way to the capital. Or, from the branches of the tree from which the seed that proved this birch once fell hung the body of a man whose feet had been burned with fire, whose genitals savaged.

The forest is not a biddable place. Comes the harrow.

It is comforting to think of the forest as a thread, thread of wood, one among many, this weaving into immanence. Casting pardon, and not always to speak.

We make patterns in language as smiths strike nails: heat, draw, hammer. Language is like a house after a fire, its halo of iron and lead. Or: like a beautiful dress with the needles and pins left in. Or: like a beautiful dress made of lead, after a fire.

The reason the angels are deaf is so that words spoken in greatest ecstasy or despair might reach God alone. The reason the angels are blind is to discourage their thieving instincts.

In the forest, theft is accomplished without reference to the senses. Xylem, phloem, photosynthesis. Ligature, fold. Theft is structure.

In the oldest stories, prayer is the fire by which the hero consumes the heroine. It is the field after the forest has been felled, also the instrument for the preparation of that field. It is an implement of teeth and of the spaces between teeth. A mangle and a map.

What love permits, in the end, is not the dispersal of the echo, but the dispersal of the hero. See him disappear into the forest piece by piece, into his palaces of celluloid and wax.

Prayer says: if you hang a new door I will batter it down. If you batter down the door I hang I will seal you in.

Prayer says: I am the residue of love.

Theft is structure. The forest is not a biddable place. Whispers paper birch and nightingale, the mistral and the sparrow, frail anemone. Comes the harrow.

RORY WATERMAN

ST. THOMAS'S

It's rock reconstituted on the rock,
order cut from the ground.
Three beeches sway eternally;
the path is soft with leaves
and bats wheel round and slice and swoop
from yew to nook to eave.
Over the fields a stub of moon
smudges the scudding cloud.

And an owl is pinned to that cloud, until it's not.
No screech will let you know
a kill's been made. Death is small
and practical, in the shadow,
where thistles thrust their pinnacles
each way: at the hedgerow,
the Milky Way, the lop-toothed huddle
of graves, the wilted window.

And you are scattered between that window and hedge –
though who can say? Ash
is finer than earth. And as the wind
stalls and blows, you must
be shifting where the owl was pinned,
and round the yews and beeches,
pirouetting on graves, out of reach,
where dust is piled on dust.

LAURA GRACE WELDON

OVERHEARD CALLS

The ordinary is mysterious to me.

How plants breathe out
what we need to breathe in
and how their leaves eat sunlight.
How radio waves careen
through buildings and bodies
making invisible fields speak.
How songs play
over and over in our heads,
a gift of memory
from ancestors who heard music
only as it was performed.
How we argue over eternity
because what's living
grows old and dies,
while styrofoam cups
and car tires persist beyond us.

NAOMI WELLS

BE WITH ME, MY DARLING LOVE, UNTIL THE WATERS COVER THE SEA

I

Aren't devout servants wished by our Sovereign Lord?
How obedient is marked rebellion?
Then why subject reluctant chastity, so fraud?
I wish to admire but one Creation
And in so doing – worship its Creator.
Too young for marriage are we, by elders, deemed –
Intent to be a dusty room's curators.
Now it is less important than it seemed –
This white band of metal is freely given.
If this law's to prevent promiscuity,
Then know that my desire is by love, driven –
For I know that I shall love you faithfully.
Be assured that I will know no other thus,
And by this act with you – I secure my trust.

II

It's considered and outdated tradition,
Yet still one that resonates in my heart –
It's part of my faith – making it part of me.
By understanding, my doubts, your worth is proved:
Respecting, conserving and even loving
My decision – despite your own frustration.
My heart is set, I'm yours 'till death us do part –
Even if yours changes, mine will constant be.
None can take your place, nor make my heart so moved
By a single touch, word or by saying nothing.

Dead would my heart be without you, my sun, my star;
Our parting, my heart, would permanently scar.
So Love, don't leave me but come away tonight –
Forget the world – for together, we are right.

ANNE WELSH

MIDWINTER

This year I don't know how to find
the way to Christmas. Instead
my mind replays memories
I'd thought to burn – the fist-blows
of my youth.
               And yet Christmas
and my family will come;
have already begun their journey South,
and there is solace in that, and comfort

that the Solstice fires warm equally
the May Queen and her sacrificial lamb,

and as the old year ends, I shall not know
the which I am – feel only this cold.

SARAH WESTCOTT

FAITH SONG

Faith in the fern's uncurling fronds,
        the specificity of cuticles
radial spokes of Scots Pine
          and the axial neurons of a lamb,
the anemone closing over a finger,
          the multiplicity and dazzle of a rock pool.

Faith in shifting sheets of sea,
        the depth and drag, the tonnage,
in flickering chains of starling
         breaking over roofs,
in songs and shapes of promise,
         light as cloud, precious as shanty.

Faith in our heavy, beautiful hands,
         their matter and their freight.

ROWAN WILLIAMS

DOOR

Lift the stone and you will find me;
Split the wood and I am there (Gospel of Thomas)

A book falling open, the sliced wood
peels apart, jolting for a moment
over the clenched swollen muscle:
so that, as the leaves fall flat
side by side, what we read is the two
ragged eyes each side of a mirror,
where the wrinkles stream off sideways,
trail down the cheeks, awash with tears,
mucus, mascara. *Split the wood*
and I am there, says the unfamiliar
Lord, there where the book opens
with the leaves nailed to the wall
and the silent knot resolved by surgery
into a mask gaping and staring, reading
and being read. Split the wood; jolt
loose the cramp, the tumour, let the makeup run,
the sap drain, the door swing in the draught.

CLIVE WILMER

DAWN CHORUS

The intervals are disproportionate.
The different melodies are overlaid.
No harmony – and yet the sounds are sweet
And of this discord all that is is made.

CHRISTIAN WIMAN

PRAYER

For all
the pain

passed down
the genes

or latent
in the very grain

of being;
for the lordless

mornings,
the smear

of spirit
words intuit

and inter;
for all

the nightfall
neverness

inking
into me

even now,
my prayer

is that a mind
blurred

by anxiety
or despair

might find
here

a trace
of peace.

KAREN WINTERBURN

SURRENDER

Come and take me
   without metaphor, my God,
    stark and bare against my questions:
Shut my mouth.

Wrap tight and dense
   around me your fierce dark;
    board up all the windows, drape the mirrors:
Put out my eyes.

Run me through
   both head and heart
    with your cold and sharp apophatic blade:
Seize my breath.

Pierce, dissolve
   the white and glaring
    bone of self I cannot kill:
Conquer me.

RODNEY WOOD

THIS WORLD TOO WILL PASS

I blame the movement of tectonic plates:
the Amurian, Bird's Head, Caroline, Manas,
Easter, Kula, North Bismark, Nazia, Cocos,
       Scotia, Juan de Fuca and more.

They've been slipping and sliding where
I live: whole roads, railway lines, canals
and airports are no longer found on the map
       and nothing points to heaven.

I visited my childhood home but it had
vanished and left a note saying it's moved
to warmer climes. My old school's replaced
       by high spec four storey flats.

My certainties, everything familiar, destroyed
but I know that one day I shall rise from my bed
and see the dazed and dreadful face of God
       waking me to another life.

CAROLYNE WRIGHT

SNOW BEFORE SLEEP: A REFLECTION IN WINTER

You must desire Nothing – Saint John of the Cross

Light glows off the drifts
like a child's long gaze upwards.
Only the sky is heavy, a drum full
of laundry – white, reluctantly tumbling.
I don't need to look out the window

to know how the corners of houses
give themselves away, like people
who'd do anything for love.
I don't glance where the snow-shagged hemlocks
sag, like the arms of saints

who have given up in prayer.
All night I refrain from gazing
while snow gathers like a last recourse
and the stripped elm limbs
lift against a sky

that cannot help itself for falling.
I don't ask for assurance. All day
I watch children jump into the drifts
as into fallen laundry, fill acres
with blank-faced angels,

the hugest possible wings.
How they can erase themselves
by how they mark the snow.
Now, clean white bandages keep dropping
from the eaves. The angel shadows

fill. No matter what I say,
snow is between us
and what we wanted to happen,
a distance that won't let us
give ourselves away.

Who else can trust that distance
the way saints trusted the down-drift
of invisible light? Its arrival
so gradual that waiting kept its habit
long after they'd relinquished prayer.

ATTALIA YAACOV-HAI

TO GLORY IN A CROWN

It had been a day of fringe trims and old lady perms. A four-year-old had kicked her way through a blow-dry a passer-by might have heard as a chainsaw massacre. I was contemplating a change in career – sheep shearing, perhaps hedge art (at least if they fuss, they do it in tones nonsensical to man) – before the jangle of the door announced: 'Do you have any free appointments today for a wash, colour and style?' I practically threw my scissors at her head. And that was before I saw what I was to be working with. I asked her to let down her hair, and when she did it fell with a heavy sigh down her back as if her head no longer had the strength to contain it, as if liberated of the burden of keeping it secret. I was reminded of my studies of Renaissance art and what it meant to have a woman's hair flow long and free: the simultaneous blatant sexualisation and metaphorical romantic connotation and the simple worship of beauty unbound. Threads of gold almost glared the light into my eyes, its mass daring me to lay a hand to it, to taint it by association. Ringlets caressed her face, punctuation to the expressions voiced by her features as she requested her multiple edits: several shades darker and lighter than her own to sew through, one to catch every type of light and toy it against the other; a fringe to sweep dramatically, cryptically across the tops of her eyes; and layers to curl their own separate stories. She was my masterpiece: I was a painter, tailor, sculptor; she was my muse as well as model. It took me several hours. When I was finished, she beamed at me through the mirror, before she stood up and began to redress her head with her Hijab. I watched as every last strand was tidily tucked away and it was almost as if I had imagined it all. I felt the absurd urge to wink at her. Instead, I turned to sweep the rest of her hair from the floor. I heard the chime of the door as she left and the mutter of someone from behind me, 'what a waste'. And I thought to myself, Yes, it would be a waste wouldn't it; to possess something beautiful and to not grant people the freedom to judge you by it.

JEFFREY YANG

FROM YENNECOTT

Alone in the woods
near running brooke, far
from wind, shelter built
pyramid of bark
leaves, saplings
provisions set
for the known hour
light deepening late
spring's colors, his eyes
felt but hidden

★

Silence of birds and trees
silence of breath, waves
of pain beginning
silence of walking feet
silence of song
cradling belly
her voice so sweet
sap-rise, soft
bed of moss
butterfly and dragonfly wild
flowers all, root-drink

★

Sun fading, falling thru branches
pain still pain without sin
panis angelius fit panis hominum
as it was as it was

at the sacred table
breath returning
thru the door of horn
vanishes on swift wings
thru the ivory door

★

Cirkell of fiere
embers floating to stars
divine spark inside
breathing   breathing
I am coming, Mesingw
is coming
I am here

★

Beaver appeared, then otter, muskrat,
toad on a lily-lotus, turtle's
slow search earth rocked
tectonic web, spider's net
Mesingw astride deer
face red black mask
eponym of peace, of
silence, steps, breath
making the forest
opening the path
Thoughts born of words:
You are not myself
nor any other
we are: thoughts

★

Surrounded by water and darkness
immersed in the sound of her heart
If this is blindness what is sight?
Before memory

      ★

They walked toward me from a great distance
and clothed me in garments of sun
faces so familiar, from a city of bridges
city of stone, city of ring-roads
waterway fields
now dust motes in a sunbeam
They rubbed my back and my feet
whispered sweet words to me
brought me food and drink
So thirsty I stood
alone
as they danced around me
knowledge and acknowledged
Salt flowing down
my body, a
vessel, my
blood my water
mixing with earth
Horus not of silence or sun
but of the child
The cries in my arms

      ★

Stepped into water to wash
by dawn's first light
I carried her
she
carried

my heart un-
sequestered forest
Mesingw's breath
everything living emotion
motion in stillness
water clear as the air
was clear, the earth, my
thoughts, hers

      ★

And after many days
of water-silence, naps
and dreams,
her milk feeding my heart, her voice
gentle wind, her face blossoming sky
I returned to the village of nine houses
without a name, uprooted
not-yet-born calling me calling me
Tears of the Father

TAMAR YOSELOFF

ILLUMINATION

Gold leaf, cadmium, ochre, saffron –
indelible once set on vellum.

The monks ground azurite and lapis
for perfect blue, took care

to cleanse their hands of poison
that made words sacred.

We place our fingers against
each other's lips, a vow of silence,

sense the touch mark even after.
I am brimming with words

but none can hold that moment
when our faces, edged in gold

glinted in the water's mirror,
the invisible sun within us –

so I let them fly, lead white
against a white sky.

C. DALE YOUNG

FOURTEEN

Bless me Father, for I have sinned. It has been
six days since my last confession. I let a guy
cheat off of my science test because it made me
feel smarter. And I ignored my Mother telling me

to be home by 9:00 pm. I don't really even know
why she asks such things. And I continue to have
impure thoughts, sometimes every hour. I let a
girl kiss me, a boy, too, but we all had our clothes on.

And this may not be a sin, but I knocked Mike down
on the basketball court just as he was making a jump,
just to be able to help him up, help him back
to the locker room. His knee got twisted. It swelled

until it looked like a softball. It was so swollen.
He let me hold ice to it until his folks came.
I liked holding the ice to it. But I found myself
having impure thoughts, Father, strange thoughts.

I sat there holding the ice and staring at his knee
and up the legs of his shorts. I could see
the white edge of his jockey shorts and more.
I had to look, Father. I had to look.

Forgive me, I couldn't help it, the staring.
It was like the time last week, after the game,
when I couldn't help but watch the soap suds
under your chin just before you washed off.

I sat on a bench in my towel and watched you, the
shape of your back, your arms, your chest. I know
this is wrong, Father, watching you in the shower.
But I only watched the soap. I only watched the water.

DAVID ZIEROTH

I WANT GOD...

... or gods, Big or small, One
or all, more than me
to lean upon, give solace
(if not an entire guarantee)
let the flow of feeling
arise elsewhere and
I promise to erect homage
daily, in my garden
You nudge me at times, truly
You do, and then You vanish
taking even hope so that
the mildest insight must
suffice, its intimation of immortality
more kind than accurate...
I know even talking this way
suggests why You left
asking why I couldn't surrender
what was it I thought
I would lose, and why
I didn't think more of the gain
(if not the entire guarantee)

ACKNOWLEDGEMENTS

Eyewear Publishing is grateful to all the publishers, editors and poets who have granted us permission to let these poems appear in this anthology.

M.J. Abell's poem is from text adapted from *Ecclesiasticus* (Sirach).

Shanta Acharya's poem was previously published in *Shringara* (Shoestring Press, 2006).

Fred Andrle's poem was previously published in *What Counts* (XOXOX Press, 2013).

Jennifer Barber's poem was previously published in *Given Away* (Kore Press, 2012).

Rachael Barenblat's poem was previously published in *Waiting to Unfold* (Phoenicia Publishing, 2013).

Margo Berdeshevsky's poem was previously published by The Academy of American Poets' *Poem-A-Day* (2013).

Charles Bernstein's poem was previously published in *Recalculating* (University of Chicago Press, 2013).

Malachi Black's poem was previously published in *Storm Toward Morning* (Copper Canyon Press, 2014).

Yvonne Blomer's poem was previously published in *As if a Raven* (Palimpsest Press, 2014).

Murray Bodo's poem was previously published in *Visions and Revisions* (Tau Publishing, 2009).

Stephanie Bolster's poem was previously published in *The City We Share* (Shoreline, 2011).

Jemma Borg's poem was previously published in *Oxford Poets Anthology 2007* (Carcanet, 2007) and *I am twenty people!* (Enitharmon, 2007).

David Briggs' poem was previously published in *Rain Rider* (Salt, 2013).

Traci Brimhall's poem was previously published in *Our Lady of the Ruins* (W.W. Norton, 2012).

Diana Bryden's poem was previously published in *Learning Russian* (Mansfield Press, 2000).

April Bulmer's poem was previously published in *Woman of the Cloth* (Black Moss Press, 2013).

Stephen Burt's poem was previously published in *Belmont* (Graywolf, 2013).

Kimberly Campanello's poem was previously published in *Consent* (Doire Press, 2013).

Ayesha Chatterjee's poem was previously published in *The Clarity Of Distance* (Bayeux Arts, 2011).

Alfred Corn's poem was previously published in *Tables* (Press 53, 2013).

Tony Curtis' poem was previously published in *Crossing Over* (Seren Books, 2007).

Grahame Davies' poem was previously published in *Lightning Beneath the Sea* (Seren, 2012).

Josephine Dickinson's poem was previously published in *Silence Fell* (Houghton Mifflin Harcourt, 2007).

Edward Doegar's poem was previously published in *Ten: The New Wave* (Bloodaxe, 2014).

Timothy Donnelly's poem was previously published in *Twenty-Seven Props for a Production of Eine Lebenszeit* (Grove Press, 2003).

Susan Millar Dumars' poem was previously published in *The God Thing* (Salmon Poetry, 2013).

Annie Finch's poem was published in *Spells: New and Selected Poems* (Wesleyan University Press, 2013).

Philip Fried's poem was previously published in *Quantum Genesis* (Zohar, 1997).

John Glenday's poem was previously published in *Undark* (Peterloo Poets, 1995).

Susan Glickman's poem was previously published in *The Smooth Yarrow* (Signal Editions of Véhicule Press, 2012).

Kim Goldberg's poem was previously published in *Ride Backwards on Dragon* (Leaf Press, 2007).

Catherine Graham's poem was previously published in *Her Red Hair Rises with the Wings of Insects* (Wolsak & Wynn, 2013).

Vona Groarke's poem was previously published in *X* (Gallery Press, 2014).

Philip Gross' poem was previously published in the essay 'If God…: Three Experiments in Poetry' in *Friends Quarterly* (2013).

Eve Grubin's poem was previously published in *Morning Prayer* (The Sheep Meadow Press, 2005).

Katia Grubisic's poem was previously published in *What if red ran out* (Goose Lane Editions, 2008).

Kevin Higgins' poem was previously published in *The New Planet Cabaret Anthology* (Ed. Dave Lordan, New Island Books, 2013).

Norbert Hirschhorn's poem was previously published in *Monastery of the Moon* (Dar-El-Javeed, Beirut, 2012).

Anthony Howell's poem was previously published in *Inside the Castle* (Barrie & Rockliffe, 1969).

Troy Jollimore's poem by permission of *MARGIE* / Intuit House.

Tess Jolly's poem was first published in *Mslexia*.

Jill Jones' poem was previously published in *The Beautiful Anxiety* (Puncher & Wattmann, 2014).

Ilya Kaminsky's poem was previously published in *Dancing in Odessa* (Tupelo, 2004).

Yahia Lababidi's poem was previously published in *Balancing Acts: New and Selected Poems* (Press 53, 2016).

Phillis Levin's poem was first published in *Poetry* and appears in *Mr. Memory & Other Poems* (Penguin Books, 2016).

Pippa Little's poem was previously published in *The Snow Globe* (Red Squirrel Press, 2011).

Helen Lovelock-Burke's poem was previously published in *Dayship* (Mulfran, 2011).

Rob Mackenzie's poem was commissioned for a digital exhibition of poems and images from Scottish and African writers by the StAnza International Poetry Festival, St Andrews, 2013.

Kathryn Maris' poem was previously published in *God Loves You* (Seren, 2013).

Jake Marmer's poem was previously published in *Jazz Talmud* (Sheep Meadow Press, 2012).

Nancy Mattson's poem was previously published in *Finns and Amazons* (Arrowhead, 2012).

Susan McCaslin's poem was published in *The Disarmed Heart* (St. Thomas Poetry Series, 2014).

Stephen Morrissey's poem was previously published in *Mythology* (Ekstasis Editions, 2014).

Karthika Nair's poem was previously published in *Bearings* (HarperCollins India, 2009).

Jan Owen's poem was previously published in *Light and Glorie* (Pantaenus Press, 2012).

Ruth Padel's poem was previously published in *Learning to Make an Oud in Nazareth* (Random House, 2014).

Molly Peacock's poem was previously published in *Alphabetique: Tales from the Lives of the Letters* (McClelland and Stewart/Random House, 2014).

Concetta Principe's poem was previously published in *Walking: Not-a-Nun's Diary,* Punchy Poetry Series (DC Books, 2013).

Susan Rich's poem was previously published in *Cloud Pharmacy* (White Pine Press, 2014).

Michael Symmons Roberts' poem was previously published in *The Half Healed* (Cape, 2008).

Antionette Voûte Roeder's poem was previously published in *Still Breathing* (Apocryphile Press, 2010).

Jerome Rothenberg's poem was previously published in *A Book of Witness* (New Directions, 2003).

Thaddeus Rutkowski's poem was previously published in *White and Wong* (BoneWorld Publishing, 2007).

Eva Salzman's poem was previously published in *Double Crossing: New and Selected Poems* (Bloodaxe, 2004).

Robyn Sarah's poem was previously published in *Pause for Breath* (Biblioasis Press, 2009).

Denise Saul's poem was previously published in *House of Blue* (Rack Press, 2012).

Jacob Scheier's poem was previously published in *Letter from Brooklyn* (ECW Press, 2013).

Michael Schmidt's poem was previously published in *Resurrection of the Body* (Smith Doorstop, 2010).

Myra Schneider's poem was previously published in *The Door to Colour* (Enitharmon Press, 2014).

Richard Scott's poem was previously published in his pamphlet *Wound* (Rialto, 2016).

Sudeep Sen's poem was previously published in *Ladakh* (Gallerie, 2012) & *Fractals: New & Selected Poems | Translations 1980-2015* (London Magazine Editions, 2016).

Don Share's poem was previously published in *Wishbone* (Black Sparrow Books, 2012).

Sandy Shreve's poem was previously published in her chapbook *Level Crossing* (The Alfred Gustav Press, 2012).

Martha Silano's poem was previously published in *Reckless Lovely* (Saturnalia Books, 2014).

Kathryn Simmonds' poem was previously published in *The Visitations* (Seren, 2013).

Floyd Skloot's poem was previously published in *Selected Poems: 1970-2005* (Tupelo Press, 2008).

Tara Skurtu's poem was previously published in *Plume*.

Elizabeth Spires' poem was previously published in *Poetry*.

Liane Strauss' poem was previously published in *Leaving Eden* (Salt, 2010).

Sean Street's poem was previously published in *Cello* (Rockingham, 2013).

Cole Swensen's poem was previously published in *Gravesend* (University of California Press, 2012).

Margo Swiss' poem was previously published in *The Hatching of the Heart* (Wipf and Stock, 2015).

Maria Taylor's poem was previously published in *Melanchrini* (Nine Arches Press, 2012).

Helen Tookey's poem was previously published in *Missel-Child* (Carcanet, 2014).

Robert Vas Dias' poem was previously published in *The Wolf*.

Jeffrey Yang's poem was previously published in *Vanishing-Line* (Graywolf Press, 2011).

Carolyne Wright's poem was previously published in *Image*.

Sarah Westcott's poem was previously published in the *Days of Roses* anthology (2011).

Tamar Yoseloff's poem was previously published in *Fetch* (Salt, 2007).

C. Dale Young's poem was previously published in *Torn* (Four Way Books, 2011).

Father Oliver Brennan holds a PhD from
Fordham University where he serves as an
Adjunct Professor of Religious Studies. He is
also a Parish Priest in the Archdiocese of Armagh.
He is the author of *Critical Issues in Religious
Education* (Veritas, 2004) and *Cultures Apart?
The Catholic Church and Contemporary Irish Youth*
(Veritas, 2001).

•

Dr. Todd Swift, Founder and Director
of Eyewear Publishing, is a poet and critic.
He is the author of many volumes of poetry,
most recently *Madness & Love in Maida Vale*.

•

Kelly Davio is the Senior Poetry Editor
of Eyewear Publishing and the Poetry
Editor of *Tahoma Literary Review*. She is the
author of the poetry collection *Burn This House*,
published by Red Hen Press.

•

Cate Myddleton-Evans is a poet and
Poetry Editor of Eyewear Publishing.
A graduate of Cambridge University,
she has studied at The Poetry School.

•

Dr. Ewan Fernie is a scholar and writer who
holds a Chair at The Shakespeare Institute,
University of Birmingham. His books include
*Redcrosse: Remaking Religious Poetry for Today's
World*, *The Demonic: Literature and Experience*, and
a Shakespeare-inspired novel coauthored with
Simon Palfrey.